"This is a book that many will be putting into their pockets and carrying with them to inspire them on a daily basis. This is a book that not only inspires, but reminds us to come back to ourselves. This is a book that reminds us of the inner connection that powers this world of reality. This is a book that is a gift of hope during a time of great change on the planet. Celeste Yacoboni has planted a seed to awaken our memory! Let our hearts unify as we celebrate our diversity and the spiritual nature we walk with."

—JYOTI, SPIRITUAL DIRECTOR FOR THE CENTER FOR SACRED STUDIES AND AMBASSADOR TO THE INTERNATIONAL COUNCIL OF THIRTEEN INDIGENOUS GRANDMOTHERS

"Celeste's book is not just entertaining, or interesting, or inspiring. It's positively revolutionary."

—ARJUNA ARDAGH, *THE TRANSLUCENT REVOLUTION*

"In this dazzling collection of praises to the One, an array of spiritual practitioners share intimate glimpses into their inner lives. What a privilege! What stunning beauty, naked humility, startling insight. This is no standard collection of established devotions; it is a full-bodied, broken-openhearted love song to the Great Mystery."

—MIRABAI STARR, *GOD OF LOVE: A GUIDE TO THE HEART OF JUDAISM, CHRISTIANITY & ISLAM*

"Celeste Yacoboni is the curator of the world's greatest spiritual practices and prayers, all put together in one beautiful, holy book and place, where anybody who believes in anything or nothing can reconnect to themselves, to God, and to why they are really here."

—MARCIA WIEDER, CEO/FOUNDER OF DREAM UNIVERSITY

"If you want to learn how to be more creative, study Leonardo da Vinci or Thomas Edison. If you'd like to improve your cooking skill, watch Michael Symon or Cat Cora on "Iron Chef." And if you want to enrich your inner life, immerse yourself in the beautiful examples of prayer from spiritual teachers, visionaries and thought leaders in this exquisite volume. *How Do You Pray?* offers creative inspiration and rich nourishment for all seekers."

—MICHAEL J. GELB, *HOW TO THINK LIKE LEONARDO DA VINCI*
AND *INNOVATE LIKE EDISON*

"Prayer is our most universal and yet also individual way of communicating with the divine, of connecting with the infinite dimension of our being. As this collection so beautifully illustrates, we each have our own way of prayer and praise. Let these words speak and remind you of this sacred mystery. Allow yourself to be drawn into this living secret of divine love."

—LLEWELLYN VAUGHAN-LEE, PH.D., SUFI TEACHER AND AUTHOR

"Each humble seeker will discern the language of prayer, the language of the heart, in his or her own way, guided by the Love that interpenetrates all existence. Nonetheless, we are richly fed and inspired by the words and witness of others in their explorations and practice within this mysterious and ultimately ordinary domain. In this feast of a book, Celeste Yacoboni presents us with dozens of invitations to stop, to listen, to let go, to wonder, to shout in praise, to cry with longing. Here is a gift for all lovers of God, whatsoever Name is assigned to that One."

—REGINA SARA RYAN, *PRAYING DANGEROUSLY* AND *IGNITING THE INNER LIFE*

"*How Do You Pray* is a rich tapestry of the ways in which people communicate with the Absolute, however it is named. It beautifully portrays humankind's eternal desire for transcendence. This book is a loving accomplishment—more like a prayer than a book."

—LARRY DOSSEY, MD, *ONE MIND: HOW OUR INDIVIDUAL MIND IS PART OF A GREATER CONSCIOUSNESS AND WHY IT MATTERS*

how do you pray?

Inspiring Responses from Religious Leaders,
Spiritual Guides, Healers, Activists
& Lovers of Humanity

Edited by Celeste Yacoboni

Foreword by Mirabai Starr

Monkfish Book Publishing

Rhinebeck, New York

How Do You Pray?
Inspiring Responses from Religious Leaders, Spiritual Guides,
Healers, Activists & Lovers of Humanity
© 2014 Celeste Yacoboni

Library of Congress Cataloging-in-Publication Data

How do you pray? : religious leaders, spiritual guides, healers, activists, and other lovers of humanity celebrate the spirit that unites us / edited by Celeste Yacoboni.
    pages cm
 ISBN 978-1-939681-17-1 (hardcover) -- ISBN 978-1-939681-23-2 (trade paper) -- ISBN 978-1-939681-18-8 (ebook)
 1. Prayer. I. Yacoboni, Celeste, editor of compilation.
 BL560.H75 2014
 204'.3--dc23
                              2013051095

Cloth ISBN: 978-1-939681-17-1
Paperback ISBN: 978-1-939681-23-2
Ebook ISBN: 978-1-939681-18-8

Book and cover design by Danielle Ferrara (aka Poor Waldo)

Monkfish Book Publishing
22 E. Market St., Suite 304
Rhinebeck, New York 12572

Dedicated to my parents Millie and Joseph,
whose love brought me to life;
and to my husband Mark, the love of my life.

acknowledgments

I bow to the Mystery that revealed itself as the vision for this book. The inquiry: *How do you pray?* has deepened my life. I am so grateful for all the prayers that have been said and sent to me. The ones in this book and the ones that aren't. And to the seeds that have been planted in our hearts and not yet spoken. I express my deep appreciation to my guides, mentors, friends and family who have inspired and supported me in ways knowing and unknowing. Though I won't name them all here, I hold them dear in my heart. I am filled with gratitude for the book's contributors who generously shared the voices of their hearts and souls so openly and tenderly.

And I express my deep appreciation to:

Paul Cohen, my publisher at Monkfish, who in his first email shared how his own vision was in alignment with *How Do You Pray?* and answered my prayer for the right publisher to bring this book out to the world;

My editor, Anastasia McGhee, for her depth of presence, patience, skill and support;

Danielle Ferrara, for the cover and layout and so much more;

Colin Rolfe, for the finishing touches;

Susan Slotter, my angel's angel, who midwifed the birth of this vision from start to finish in a multitude of creative and technical roles, and held every aspect as sacred and brought that sacredness into form;

My soul coach, Patricia Flasch, who held the vision from the beginning and wrote the very first contribution;

Multidimensional thinker Michael Gelb, whose laser perception and guidance focused my intention, which has manifested in this book;

Nancy Andersen, who took my vision and created the original sanctuary website;

Marco Britt, for evolving the website and being of service;

Jason Rodriguez, for his creativity with the visual book;

Photographer Jennifer Esperanza, whose many photos illustrated the prayers and whose photo of a little girl praying captured the purity of the vision;

Marcia Wieder, for offering me what I needed before I even asked;

Hubert Lee, for his brilliance with marketing and promotion;

Zuleikha, for her intuition and kindness;

Mirabai Starr, who held the torch to light my way, and overflowed with support and guidance;

Andrew Harvey, for his radical honesty and recommendations;

Dunya, for our ritual of morning tea and spiritual conversation—sohbet;

Robyn Benson, for her care and for encouraging me to share;

Arjuna Ardagh and Sedena and George Cappannelli, for going the extra step;

BiBi Dietz, for her transcription wizardry;

Bob Keeton, for his audio and video genius and generosity;

Sr. Pascaline Coff and the Bede Griffiths International Literary Trust, for their support in bringing Fr. Bede Griffith's prayer to these pages;

Amritapriya and Steve Schmidt for Amma's Prayer;

Jalaluddin Rumi, Sufi mystic and poet whose words inspire me to listen and speak from my heart;

My mother Millie, who is a constant source of love, inspiration and support; the loving memory of my father Joseph, who is always with me;

My brother Ty and his wife Kathy; my brother Brian and my nephew Nic;

Lillian, my second mother and friend; children Austin and Becky and grandson Asher, who fill me with joy;

And lastly, my beloved husband Mark, who has supported me in ways too many to mention, and to whom I am forever grateful.

Our relationship to Spirit (if we are lucky) is ever-changing. Our prayer life reflects this fluidity. Sometimes our hearts spill over with gratitude and a spontaneous *thank you* billows from the cup of our souls. Or perhaps our hearts are shattered by loss and in our free fall we cry out for the compassionate arms of an all-loving Divine being. At these times, the existence of a Creator seems obvious and we are certain that the Big Plan makes sense and that our only job is to say *yes*. At other times, the notion of a personified Deity seems childish, even delusional, and we fire God and replace him with an amorphous yet sacred suchness. We consider this formless holiness to be unnamable, but we can't help naming it a little bit: Ultimate Reality, maybe, or Buddha Nature, the interconnected web of being or the great mystery.

I used to think I had to pick one and stick with it. I needed either to believe in a God I could love and long for, confide in and argue with, or else transcend all such dualistic concepts and forge a direct relationship with my source, with which I am already and forever one (in spite of appearances). In Christian mystical terms, this is the distinction between *cataphatic* and *apophatic* theology. The cataphatic approach is to define and personalize God by naming all his positive attributes, which leads to a state of worship and adoration of the Divine as Wholly Other. The apophatic way is to acknowledge that any attempt to speak of the Divine is a limitation, because God is an undifferentiated unity, which defies all description and surpasses all understanding.

Well, guess what: we don't have to choose. We can be true believers and agnostics at the same time, equally dedicated to contemplative practice and devotional rituals, in love with science and in awe of the Unseen. We can reach out to a loving God in desperation and in thanksgiving, and we can also rest in the boundless, take refuge in the formless, melt back into our True Self. There is no contradiction here. Rather, it is a reflection of the paradoxical nature of the spiritual life: we are both separate from and in union with our Beloved. We yearn to return, and we have never been apart. At the heart of all the world's religious traditions and spiritual paths, we find affirmation of this singular truth.

Celeste Yacoboni is a luminous exemplar of the tribe of interspiritual beings that is quietly coalescing all over the planet. For Celeste, there is no meaningful difference between Catholic and Quaker, Sikh and Sioux, neurobiologist and Chasidic Jew. Celeste is endowed with the gift of an interspiritual heart, and equally charged with the task of conveying our essential oneness to a world ravaged by religious strife. Celeste is a healer, and by compiling these diverse responses to the simple question, "How do you pray?" she brings healing to us all.

The diversity of voices Celeste has gathered in these pages reflects the dynamic reality of the many ways we are called home to the One. Some of the writers are unapologetically religious, and have a juicy personal relationship with God. Some relate to the Divine as the mysterious holiness that pervades and connects all that is, but would prefer not to personify it. Others deny the existence of what could be called God, yet their inner lives are a source of sanctuary from which they draw sustenance to be of better service. All seem to affirm that the natural outflow of prayer is compassionate action, and that to cultivate a solitary connection with the Divine is to participate in a collective spirituality that uplifts the whole world.

Here's my prayer: that you, like me, find guidance, inspiration and fresh new ways of connecting to Spirit amid the array of prayers and accounts collected here. May you, like me, discover that some days you are a theist and some days a pantheist, and that there is nothing wrong with this. Sometimes your God is Father, sometimes Mother, sometimes Lover. Maybe you also encounter the Holy One in pure emptiness and speak to the Holy One without words. How you pray might change as the chapters of your life unfold, tragedy by tragedy, blessing by blessing, moment by moment. Underneath the shifting story is this other thing—this great secret, this deep stillness, this ecstatic song—in the face of which all we can do is fall to our knees, in wonderment and bewilderment, and praise and fall silent.

—Mirabai Starr, August 2013

How do *you* pray? Is it an hour a week at a designated place of worship or do you take your prayers out to the streets? Do you pray like your parents, culture or tribe or have you found another way? Do you pray to God or do you have another special name or no name at all? Is it a monologue or a conversation or neither? How does your soul express itself when you are in need and how does that differ from your expression when you feel fulfilled?

Do you dance in ecstasy? Bare your soul to the divine?

Bow in gratitude? Merge with nature? Cry out for guidance?

As a minister, healer and seeker for many years, my understanding is that we are one people united in our divine source, with so many beautiful names. My calling has been to awaken others to the realization that our oneness is our greatness.

As darkness turned to light early one morning in 2008, it dawned on me that the question "How do you pray?" was to determine the direction of my life. A compelling inner voice asked me if I was prepared to bring this question to the world. When I arose, I awakened to a profound sense that deep contemplation of this simple question was a means to both celebrate diversity and highlight our unity. As I came in touch with people throughout the day and looked into their eyes I felt the words emerge from my heart: How do you pray?

Over time, I came to feel that a book filled with people's answers to that question, all sharing from their hearts how they pray, would be a service to anyone who seeks a richer inner life. I first asked my family, friends and mentors for their stories. They were deeply touched and willing to share. I then reached out far and wide and the responses poured in.

So deep, honest and generous are the prayers collected in these pages that I bow in gratitude to all who wrote them as well as to all of us who read and are inspired by them. The contributions in this book come from many different spiritual paths, including no path at all, but as you read them you'll experience a sense of resonance and alignment.

Whether the essays were written by people who are religious, or 'spiritual but not religious', or some other category altogether, they all share the common thread of a love for humanity. Most responses were written especially for this book, but when invited, some people really wanted to be part of it and had the perfect contribution already written and previously published. Artists and photographers sent me visual prayers, or a combination of words and images.

The way we pray provides a mirror to our soul. It reflects our most fundamental values and beliefs, hopes and dreams, fears and doubts. Prayer unifies us with ourselves and with each other by putting us in touch with the divine essence within. *How Do You Pray?* embodies this essence with deep personal sharing by a remarkably diverse group of people, including some of the most beloved teachers of our time. And it comes at an auspicious moment. We are giving birth to a new spirituality. We are finding the strength to leave behind beliefs that no longer serve us, all the while honoring our traditions. We are discovering a oneness that includes and celebrates our diversity. We are evolving a new perspective that integrates old and new, traditional and alternative, individual and collective. This new approach is grounded in appreciation and gratitude for all who came before us, and in responsibility and preparation for those yet to come.

How Do You Pray? is intended to offer guidance, support and inspiration. Imagine as you read the prayers of the 129 people in this book that we are all part of a prayerfield, an energetic flow of love for each other, for our Earth, and for the Divine. I suggest first reading the book straight through. The journey is transformational and you may stop and rest along the way. Then you can intuitively let the book fall open and contemplate the entry. You may sit with your favorites often, and explore and get to know those less familiar.

In the back of the book you will find short biographies of the contributors, which are arranged alphabetically by author. Reading their bios will help you connect with the people behind the prayers and offers a bountiful resource of council, exploration and community. My prayer for you is that as you enjoy the prayers of others, you'll discover your own truest prayers, and thus a deeper connection to your divine essence.

—Celeste Yacoboni, April 2014

how do you pray?

Let's start with the definition of prayer, the most classical definition that you learn in Sunday School: "the lifting up of heart and mind to God." It is not saying prayers, obviously; it is not even an action doing this or doing that. It is an attitude, an attitude of lifting up heart and mind to God. So, start the other way around and ask, "What lifts up your heart and mind? What gives you a lift?"

You might say, "Well, for me it's fishing. Fishing gives me a lift." That's wonderful then—fishing is your primary prayer, as long as you do it in an open-hearted way. As long as you let it do something to you, rather than you grasping something with it. This is very often the case with people who go fishing. It seems to me, as I watch them sitting there fishing, that they are often just as meditative as people who sit by the Ganges River without a fishing rod. I get the impression that this fishing rod is just an excuse for sitting by the river and meditating. I wouldn't be surprised if in many cases it was really a very deep prayer.

But there may be something else that lifts up your heart and mind to God. Whatever lifts up your heart, focus on that. Ask yourself, "How does that feel?" and "Why does it come about?" Very frequently it will come about because it raises in you a sense of gratefulness. If that is the case, then do whatever you do not consider prayer—what does not lift up your heart and mind to God— gratefully, or joyfully, or with an open heart, or whatever the essence of your prayer is. Then it will be prayer.

When I am able I pray with my feet. I walk the farm between the cedar trees. I cross the creek on the flat rocks to sit on an island of bluebells and look back across the water where I have been. Holy are the ways given to us all to travel. I eat the food I have grown, the seeds I have prayed over as they entered the ground.

How do I pray? I go to stand in the temples inside the sanctuaries of ancient places where many lived and died, and believed that Light and Love were not only possible, but were embodied here and now. I stand in the midst of all that and remember that we came from stardust, and that dust is made from dissolving. I pray to be awake to the Divine and to Love at all times.

How do I pray? I rise before dawn. I sit at my desk and stare out at the eastern hill. As the sun rises, the sunlight behind the hills causes the trees to become like wicks that hold a candle flame. The world ignites before my eyes. I put my pen to the paper and I write.

At night, when day is done, I go out into the backyard, sometimes wrapped in a blanket, and stand beneath the stars. I stare up at Orion, the Pleiades, Cassiopeia. I send what is in my heart out to the center of the universe. I imagine myself as one light linked to a thousand celestial fires. For all of this, I am deeply grateful.

How do I pray? I say I love you.

Trans-Substantiation

In the morning I wake
inside green tents of light
cast down by maple trees.
Isis breathes next to me.

I walk into a cathedral of trees
amid the choir of birds and wind,
amid dripping leaves and rushing creek.

normandi ellis

Isis sings in the morning air.
I feel the breath of my family
stirring up from their blankets,
filling the teacups and billowing the curtains
with their powerful dreams.
Isis dreams through and inside them.

The Earth is a prayer rug;
my coffee cup—a common chalice.
The rising sun is a wafer of light ...

Take. Eat. This is my Body.
Do this and Remember Me.

Prayer to me is waking up each morning and giving gratitude for the miracle of my life and the life of all living beings that are connected to the web of life.

I pray by giving thanks and gratitude to earth, air, water and fire and the sun for giving me all that I need to thrive.

I give thanks for the love of the universe, with God/the goddess knowing that I am being supported through the good times and the challenges that lead to my growth and evolution.

Prayer for me is a way of life that is not separate from each breath and each step I take on this great Earth.

I pray for others and the Earth by seeing all in its divine light, lifting all who I pray for into radiance.

Our food is a gift from the world. We are invited to eat it mindfully. And if we are lucky, we are planting our gardens in the spring, and enjoying their fruits in the ripening time. At Upaya Zen Center and at our mountain retreat, the Refuge, we have beautiful gardens. We feed many people and some of what we offer our students and guests is food from our land. Before every meal, we make a food offering. This is a way of expressing our gratitude for the food before us, as well as to vow to return this gift by serving the world. The prayer is thus:

> Earth, water, fire, air and space
> combine to make this food.
> Numberless beings gave their lives and labors
> that we may eat.
> May we be nourished,
> that we may nourish life.

This meal offering was composed while walking the trails around Annapurna Mountain. I can still taste the Himalayan air and rice and dhal that graced this gorgeous journey. The words of the offering reflect the profound gratefulness I felt being able to walk those mountain passes and have the energy to make my way on pilgrimage on two good legs and with close friends.

Prayer is perhaps one of the most ancient and mysterious of human experiences. It's also one of the most personal. Even before the word "prayer" appeared in spiritual practices, the oldest records of the Christian and Gnostic traditions used words such as "communion" to describe our ability to speak with the unseen forces of the universe. Prayer is unique to everyone who experiences it. Some estimate that there are as many ways to pray as there are people who do the praying!

Today, modern prayer researchers have identified four broad categories that are believed to encompass all of the many ways that we pray. In no particular order, they are: colloquial or informal prayers, petitionary prayers, ritualistic prayers and meditative prayers. When we pray, the researchers suggest that we use one of these four modes or a combination.

As good as these descriptions are, and as well as each of these prayers appears to work, there's always been another mode of prayer that this list doesn't account for. This fifth mode of prayer, the "lost mode," is a prayer that's based solely on feeling. Rather than accompanying the sense of helplessness that often leads us to ask for assistance from a higher power, feeling-based prayer acknowledges our ability to communicate with the intelligent force that 95 percent of us believe in, and participate in the outcome.

Without any words, without our hands held in a certain position or any outward physical expression, this mode of prayer simply invites us to feel a clear and powerful feeling as if our prayers have already been answered. Through this intangible "language," we participate in the healing of our bodies, the abundance that comes to our friends and families, and the peace between nations.

I pray through poetry.

I've never had a relationship to prayer. Until recently, I couldn't fathom what people got out of reciting in Hebrew at dusk or bowing down to Allah five times a day, or repeating the Lord's Prayer or the Rosary. Then, in a moment of extreme darkness, almost by accident, I discovered the power of speaking a poem that I love, and suddenly I understood.

I spent most of my life being afraid of poetry. I felt like I didn't understand it, like it was a secret language that other people understood and I didn't. Then, in 1994, I fell into an extreme depression that was unshakeable. Even though I was a therapist and spiritual teacher at the time, none of the teachings or techniques I had access to could touch the place that felt so broken in me. Until one day I happened to hear a man reciting poems unlike any I had encountered in school. These were the poems of the inner life, the poems of Rilke and Mary Oliver, of Rumi and Kabir. Something about the words, the spaces between them and the resonance of the voice cracked me open. For the first time since the depression had gripped me, I felt release.

I became inspired to start memorizing poems myself. Very quickly I entered a much deeper, more life-changing process than I ever expected. It was as if I had inadvertently walked into an ancient mystery school. Years later, in the process of researching my book *Saved by a Poem*, I discovered that, in fact, this was true. The art of taking sacred words into one's memory was a mystical practice in both Eastern and Western traditions until at least the sixteenth century. The ancient Buddhists, who could neither read nor write, passed down the Buddha's words by learning them by heart. They called it "writing on the bones." For Plato, committing sacred words to memory was a way to align our material existence with the higher vibrations of spirit.

I discovered that there is a huge difference between memorizing and learning by heart. The first is about exercising one's will over the poem. The other is about allowing oneself to be opened and changed by the poem. As I learned more poetry by heart, healings began to unfold on all levels of my being. My body became vibrant and alive from the resonance of my own voice, the deepening of my breath, the quickening of my pulse to the rhythms of the words. My emotions, feelings, thoughts and insights were touched and shaped by the wisdom of the poems. And huge shifts happened when I started to speak poems to others. The intimacy of sharing this language of life below the surface with another person is, to me, the most precious communion. It's like praying together.

Most of the poems I speak—both to myself and to others—are written by other people. So the communion is not only among those gathered in the moment, but can resonate across history to include a person who wrote centuries ago in a language I don't know. Here is a poem I love by the German poet, Rainer Maria Rilke. It was written in 1899, but it is a prayer that touches my life almost every day:

Before We Are Made

God speaks to each of us as we are made
then walks with us silently out of the night.
These are the words, the numinous words,
we hear before we begin:

You, called forth by your senses,
Reach to the edge of your Longing:
Become my body.

Grow like a fire behind things
so their shadows spread out
and cover me completely

Let everything into you: Beauty and Terror.
Keep going: remember, no feeling is forever.

Don't lose touch with me.
Nearby is the land
they call Life.
You will recognize it
by its intensity.

Give me your hand.

This poem instantly lassoes my panicky survival driven anxiety—as
well as my habitual thought patterns—and brings me into a sanctuary
within myself. Any poem you love can be a sanctuary. Literally. A poem
can build a sacred space within you because it changes the physiological
reality within your body. The sounds and silences of a poem affect your
breathing, your pulse, even your brain waves and cerebrospinal fluid.
And when you speak the poem aloud, the sound vibrates the crystals
in your bones and fascia the way your voice vibrates in the nave of a
cathedral, creating a special resonance that invites revelation.

And it doesn't have to be a holy poem. I love the work of spiritual
poets like Rumi, Rilke, Kabir and Hafiz. But I also call on modern
poets, who may not have thought of themselves as mystical, but
who speak with such originality and depth of feeling about the
inner life that, to me, their poems are prayers. I think of poets like
Naomi Shihab Nye, Marie Howe, Leonard Cohen and W.S. Merwin.
Recently I've been falling in love with Walt Whitman. Here are a few
lines from *Leaves of Grass* that I speak to myself every day:

I exist as I am, that is enough,
If no other in the world be aware I sit content,
And if each and all be aware I sit content.
One world is aware and by far the largest to me, and that is myself,
And whether I come to my own today or in ten thousand or ten million years,
I can cheerfully take it now, or with equal cheerfulness I can wait.

My way of praying is to express gratitude as often as possible.

As a Muslim, I perform body prayers by bowing and prostrating to God in gratitude. Several times a day, in the midst of attractions and distractions, I am reminded of the need to bring God into the center of my life. Islamic sages explain that one prostration of prayer to God frees me from a thousand prostrations to my ego. I am grateful for the reminders.

In the course of my day, I find opportunity upon opportunity to express thanks by touching my heart. I have so many gifts in my life: family and friends, health and well-being, joys and surprises, sights and sounds, food and drink—an endless stream! When I give thanks, I join a cosmic chorus and feel uplifted. The Quran exults, "Whatever is in the heavens and on earth extols the limitless glory of God." (62:1). The Prophet Muhammad exclaimed that a bird, after sipping water, always tilts its head upward, not only for the water to flow through, but for praise and thanks to flow heavenward!

In times of difficulty, I persevere with my prayers of gratitude and add a special prayer taught by my Sufi teachers: "O God, save me from its harm but please do not deprive me of its good." When I continue to pray in this way in periods of affliction, I know that I am giving thanks for unknown blessings already on their way.

At nighttime I always end my nocturnal rituals with a prayer taught by my parents:

O God,
favor upon favor
have you bestowed
upon this handful of dust.
Thank you, my Sustainer.

As a Jew, I have liturgy for three, four times a day, plus many, many blessings each day—of our food, and even going to the bathroom and acknowledging that everything works—and you say a thank you prayer for that. So I have a lot of liturgical texts that some people would see as *obligations*. And I see them as *opportunities*. If I can, at the beginning of the day, I allow myself to open a prayer book and begin with a blessing over the use of the bodily functions, and then go on from there to the place of the celebration of the hallelujahs, and then go to the contemplative place of looking at the universe and at the power of the Creator and the universe, and then to the credo, and then come to the very personal requests to be made, and then from that place, slowly come down with thanksgiving for each one of the places where I was, and at the end of the session of prayer I sit down with a pencil and paper and take my orders from the God I spoke to.

People say to me sometimes, "How come my prayer isn't being answered?" and I tell them, "You hang up the phone too soon." It's necessary to sit for a while and to get the action directive, the marching orders for the day.

The best times for prayer are the twilight times, dawn and dusk, because we have the consciousness of day and night. The left brain and right brain are still meeting together in the heart, and that's a very, very good prayer time. Then we have the prayers that are in the middle of the day, that are rushed between one appointment and the other, and those are the quick arrow prayers that say, "Here, God, I'm busy with all these things; please help me."

Find a place where you don't feel that you have to worry about being overheard, and speak so that your ear can hear. If you sit there, and you begin to concentrate on the You, You, You, You, and you begin to speak about what's real—even just to say, "You, I feel so foolish talking to You because I don't see anybody here, and yet I know that I wouldn't be here if You weren't here, so I'm doing the best I can. I want to thank You for every breath that I can take. I want to thank You for my health"—that is beginning to pray.

Begin prayer with gratefulness, because that's the easiest one. We have lots to be grateful for—the fact we can see with our eyes, and we can hear, and so on. After you begin with gratitude, then comes the other stuff, the concerns: "I want to share with you my concerns, dear God. These are the people I'm concerned about. A friend of mine had an operation today. I hope she heals well." To be able to speak about concerns in this way—that will make the difference.

Piety is not just being nice. Piety is real. It's the kind of intimacy that you want to have with someone whom you love.

I so appreciate having heard, once, Terry Gross interviewing the gay bishop of New Hampshire. And she asked him, "What's your prayer life like these days?" And he said to her, "The best thing that I can do is just sit there and let God love me." I was so moved by what he shared, I sent him a fan letter right away. Because that's true—we all say, "God so loved the world, God loves me, Jesus loves me," and so on, but we hardly ever sit down and let ourselves be loved. That's become part of my practice, too.

"It is only in prayer that we can communicate with one another at the deepest level of our being. Behind all words and gestures, behind all thoughts and feelings, there is an inner center of prayer where we can meet one another in the presence of God. It is this inner center which is the real source of all life and activity and of all love. If we could learn to live from that center we should be living from the heart of life, and our whole being would be moved by love. Here alone could all the conflicts of this life be resolved, and we can experience a love which is beyond time and change."

Bede Griffiths
The Golden String
published by Templegate

How do I pray?

I never learned any traditional way to pray, so I've discovered many ways to practice. My tool kit has expanded as I've grown into a more consistent spiritual relationship with myself and with all my relations, including the land, the ancestors and the mystery. Not having been taught any spiritual rituals in my childhood has become a gift to me now, as I feel free to borrow from many sources. In this way, I have assembled my own eclectic and very personal array of options for relating to the divine, the invisible world and that which I consider sacred.

Sometimes my prayer emerges from my heart, other times from the bottom of my belly. Sometimes prayers drift in from the dream world, appear upon awakening or emerge from a vision that's ignited in my mind's eye. And sometimes they rise up from the bottoms of my feet, perhaps emerging from our universal mother and sacred home.

Sometimes my prayers are imagined inwardly, and offered silently. Sometimes they are ritualized in creativity, by writing a poem, singing a song or making a drawing. Sometimes they are murmured under my breath, and sometimes they are cawed in a dialogue with the crows that live nearby, in a language that sounds to me like theirs.

Sometimes—like the time that I was humming my prayers wordlessly as I rocked a woman having an asthma attack at 3:00 a.m. at a rural retreat center in northern New Mexico—mine is a felt prayer, experienced somatically in my body and repeated inwardly and endlessly, like: "Please, don't let her die, please let her come through this, please let her find her breath." Then responses to my prayers—in that case, instructions for what to do that might help her—come back to me through my body, too.

For me, praying is reciprocal and multi-directional. Sometimes a prayer originates within me, while at other times a prayer seems to rise up from the land or from other places outside myself. Perhaps praying is cyclical and endless, like breathing, and a continuous exchange of insight: listening and learning on the in-breath, with offerings of wishes, dreams and yearnings on the exhalation.

A Peruvian shaman named Oscar Miro Quesada taught me that "consciousness creates matter," so I take special care about how I use prayer. I remember that thoughts can seed manifestation, and so I am mindful about cultivating my own discernment and specificity when I pray. He also taught me that "language creates reality," so I try to be rigorous about the words I select to convey my prayers. Lastly, I learned from him that "ritual creates relationship," so when I care especially deeply about a prayer's outcome, or am in real need of support from the invisible world, I often invent some sort of creative way to enact or symbolize what I am praying for.

When I pray for rain, I have learned not to focus on what's missing—as if there could ever be a lack in nature—but instead to recall the sensory memory of what I long for. I remember the deliciously sweet scent of the earth just after rain in the desert, the cool delight of gentle droplets spattering on my head and skin. I appreciate nature for her resilience and bounty, and invite her to revisit us again in that generous way.

My practice is usually to begin with gratitude. I frequently begin by sending my thankfulness for the beauty, love and synchronicity that surrounds and holds me. I notice how much is mysterious and loving, how much is joyous and wildly resourceful and inspiring in my world. My heart swells in recognition of how fortunate I am, in appreciation for the wellness and complex magnificence of my body's capabilities, the love of my web of relations, the joy of living in a beautiful place and having work that makes my heart glad.

When I pray for specific things, or really care deeply about the outcome, that's when I know it's especially important that—even while I infuse my prayer with the potency of my heart's desire—I also surrender my own will up to a greater power. I recall that I cannot ever know what's truly meant to happen. I remember that even as I yearn for something, I cannot truly know what's the correct outcome. When I'm in my most mindful and centered place, I pray only that Gaia's—or the divine mystery's—will be done. And I humbly ask for help from anyone or any energy listening that may have love, gifts or guidance to offer.

jyoti

Many of us have been trained with an understanding of the sacred and its instruments. We know that the line that we are holding with our pipes goes back to the original time—the first time—that pipe was picked up and was carried. Those prayers go through all these generations, and when we light that pipe the way we've been trained, the way the pipe has asked us to take care of it, then the prayer is sitting solidly in its power for those we are praying for. We know that all of those prayers behind us show up in that moment when we light that tobacco in that pipe. It's another way of looking at the continuity of prayer. That's when you can feel the root of prayer running through all our lives. So prayer for me, as one who has been trained in traditional ways and initiated by First Nation people, is about a way of life.

And that way of life has the teachings given to us by Creation to care for life as sacred. That space, when we walk with it, offers sustainability and balance and relatedness. Those are the seeds of a true prayer. We reach into some of these places of prayer not through words, but through the place that's beyond words. Sound of some kind, such as chanting or music or breath, can take you there. Sitting on a mountaintop, being still and listening to the wind and the birds sing can take you there. Dance and mindfulness practices can put you in that state of prayer we're talking about. Prayer is not about outcome. We don't pray for outcome. We just pray.

I may be standing, sitting or lying down. There is no set form, though I like it when I am directly on the Earth. I particularly like being on grass or on a boulder or lying down looking up at a tree or at the sky. I become completely still. The rest unfolds. I do not will it to happen. I often feel both a kind of detachment and a blending—a detachment from my daily concerns and, at the same time, a blending, a oneness with the Earth and all its creatures. A state of appreciation, gladness and compassion washes through me the way the body's pulsing energies move through every cell. It is a prayerful state rather than active prayer, such as asking for something. However, in this state, sometimes someone or a longing for an outcome comes into my awareness, and I feel the person or situation infused with the passion, possibility and serenity of that prayerful state.

sobonfu somé

I pray in many different ways.
The clarity of my intention is the beginning of my prayer.

In my tradition, every breath I draw is a prayer.
Every time I inhale and exhale, it is a prayer.
And so, how conscious are you when you are breathing in and
    out?
How conscious are you when you are walking?
How conscious are you when you are singing?
How conscious are you when you are angry?
I pray in the way I show gratitude, love or compassion.
I pray alone and in community.
I pray with my thoughts.
I pray with my body.

I pray in the way I speak to people.
I pray to the various elements of nature—
    the trees, the animals, the water, the rocks, the earth, the fire....
I pray to my Ancestors and all the Divinities.
I pray simply, with passion, humility, clarity and grace.

I pray in the way I welcome and bless people.
I pray with whatever emotions come my way.
I pray with sincerity and with strong belief that what I'm
    praying for is going to manifest.

In my tradition, whatever you say is a prayer that you send out,
Because sound is a powerful force that brings the hidden to
    light.
And when you pray something is going to say Yes.

So each moment in my life is a prayer.

Each moment I reflect on myself, on the world and other people
   is a prayer.
How I interact with people and how I deal with my thoughts is
   a prayer.
How genuine am I?—is a way for me to pray.

For me, all these things are sacred and are messengers, and can
   take my heart cries, which are my prayers to the Divinities.
This is the power of how I pray.

michael gelb

Every morning I pause for a few minutes and dedicate the day to the Divine. I say the Shema, the Lord's Prayer, the Prayer of St. Francis and a Sanskrit invocation for the healing and happiness of all sentient beings. I give thanks to my ancestors and spiritual mentors.

Throughout the day, I pause every hour and renew that dedication. As Mother Meera reminds us: "Offering everything, pure and impure, is the best and quickest way to develop spirituality. It is not what you offer, but *that* you offer which is important."

I say silent grace before every meal. I review the day's blessings and forgiveness opportunities each night before I sleep. I give thanks and ask for help in forgiving and releasing any unresolved issues. I wake up the next morning and rinse and repeat.

My way of praying is through sound. Sound for me is color, is form. Sound is an expression of love. Sound is a bond with the sacred, and prayer is a bond with the sacred, an invocation. Whichever your sense of sacred is, I do it through sound.

My path with prayer, with the sacred, is through sound, and the words accompany the sound. That is part of where I have been walking in the last few years since I became a grandfather. It has allowed me to advance further and deeper into my spiritual path. Before I became a grandfather, my path was more superficial, more self-centered, the egocentric world of an artist, a writer, a painter, a musician—image comes first and then the rest. I spent a long time in that place. We artists have that problem, like intellectuals or great characters. We sin through arrogance, but I continue working to overcome this, and my condition of becoming a grandfather has helped me a great deal. Also, the profound solitude I have experienced in the last few years has brought an awakening of prayer to sound.

I have a set of thirteen musical instruments, which are thirteen prayers. I make my own musical instruments, searching for sounds that bring me closer to the sacred. And what is prayer? That which allows you to come closer to the sacred, to come closer to its inner part.

I have moments of prayer through musical instruments, which, for me, are living entities that have a spirit and through which I do my prayers. This form of praying started to come to my life through the teachings of my masters, both male and female. The sound started to develop, without words, through the musical instruments.

For instance, among the deities that we have in the Andes are the Sacred Mountains. We call them the "Apus," the Guardian Mountains of the people. With them, I pray through a conch shell trumpet, a "Potuto." When I play, I am not only making a sound, I am making a prayer. The prayer is to awaken and invoke the presence of the Apus. I am asking for protection. The words would be, "Sacred mountain, tutelar of our lives, protect life, protect our brothers..." and much more, but this happens in images through the sound.

My upbringing is Shamanic, part of the traditions of my people, but I also have a Christian upbringing, so I also pray to the Virgin of Guadalupe, who is the Virgin of my town and the feminine deity of my people. The instrument I use is the Mama Quena (Mother Flute). This is one of the most important parts of my prayer work. This Mother Flute—this Mama Quena—is a flute of great size that has a tuning characteristic particular to my people. It is a tuning that opens up the most emotive parts of your body, tuned in A minor, which is a very intuitive tuning. This is the zone in which to invoke the Mother; it is the zone in which to invoke women, including important female characters from our history: Mary Magdalene, Micaela (a great woman advocate of the tradition of Andean people and their culture). I also invoke my teacher Amelia through the Mama Quena; the Mama Quena doesn't become a song, it becomes a prayer through sound.

What do I look for through prayer? I look, in the end, to be a better person, to be a better soul, to be something good for the people who are close to me. Also, a prayer reflects on the search for a more humane world, a world with more social justice, a world with forms of deep sharing.

Does my prayer look for change? Yes. Do I pray for change? Yes. Do I pray for the world powers to have a moment of reflection in which they can look at themselves and see the profound damage they do? Yes. Is my prayer—my song—political? Yes. Is my prayer politics? Yes. Am I a political man? Yes. Do I look for change? Yes. Do I look for the political transformation of my people? Yes. Do I look for the cultures born from my people to have greater political presence? Yes. Through prayer? Yes. Through my song? Yes. I don't divorce my work from my political component. This is very controversial for many people who adopt a totally different position.

Do I believe that there is a deep inequality and much political responsibility on the world powers? Yes. Especially the great world powers? Yes. On North America? Yes. The European Union, too? Yes. Is there a cordon of extreme poverty, misery and death in the world due to excessive exploitation? Yes. Is there a profound impact in mistreating nature? Yes. Do they want to make us all the same through globalization? Yes. So, against this we also pray, but we pray with a very strong component. We pray for our center to awaken, for our power to awaken, so it makes us strong and sometimes able to say: Enough.

This is my prayer.

A Rwandan woman sits in a circle telling her story of great family loss in the genocide. She is overcome with tears. Words fail. Her grief pulls her to lie facedown on the ground. An African American woman who has dedicated her life to racial healing comes and lies down on the floor beside her, also facedown. Then a third woman, who has given most of her life to working with children of war and others who have endured great trauma, also lies down beside her. The spirits of so much hurt and wounding crowd around the three prostrate women. A Hopi elder, a grandmother, rises and prays over them with simple dignity. Light enters the story.

This is how I pray in circle after circle. I offer my heart's capacity to open. I allow the molten lava of suffering to flow through it. Then when it is ready, in silence, in stillness, this heart becomes witness to the incomparable beauty of healing. And everything within me becomes a song.

My personal prayer is the prayer of the heart—a prayer born of need and longing, an opening to the mystery of love that is always present within. It is a deep prayer of silence and love in which the heart looks towards its Beloved. For this prayer of the heart there is no time or ritual because it is the most intimate cry of the heart, when sometimes tears run down my face and my heart aches. Often in the night I lie awake, feeling a sweet pain that turns me towards the One I love. I may try to put words to this prayer, sometimes the words flow with the tenderness that lovers whisper to the one they love, and sometimes words come with anguish when I feel so separate, so abandoned, left alone with the heart's longing. But deeper than any words is the silence that calls, a silence that I need and which mysteriously also needs me.

This is the primal prayer of the soul, a merging into the emptiness that is within, that is at the very center of my heart. Here, there is a giving of myself to my Beloved with a totality that is a complete belonging to love. I feel that I am the very core of my longing, a desire that comes from the heart and embraces every breath, every cell of my body. All of my being and body is then in prayer, nothing is excluded from this prayer, this turning of the heart, this pouring out of my whole self. Every cell of the body feels this sweet anguish, the potency of this prayer of love. And I wait, hoping, longing, needing my Beloved more than I know. And then, when I feel my Beloved, when I feel that love present within, I come to know the essence of prayer, that there is no separation, that we are always together in love. This is the mystery of oneness.

There comes the time when this prayer is continuous, a prayer without ceasing, because how can the heart forget its Beloved, how can it not look towards the Source of its love and longing? Whatever moment of the day, whatever outer activities, when I look within I see this mystery that is praying, the silence and wonder of how the heart is a place of prayer, an altar of love. I feel the tenderness, the sweetness, the power of this prayer. This prayer is the essence of my being, a covenant of love, a remembrance, a meeting and a merging. It is a living oneness within me that belongs to every moment of the day and night. This prayer is my practice, an offering of myself, my own most intimate way of being with my Beloved. What else can I do in this world but pray? We are love's prayer.

zuleikha, international performer
rumi concert 2013
www.storydancer.com

The first thing I do when I wake up is to get on my knees and kiss the ground. I give thanks to God for another day, ask for the protection of the elders of my path, and sit in prayer. I put the Earth in my heart and ask that during the day I will be Her eyes and ears, so that the bird that does not know its song, the flower that does not know its smell, the fruit that does not know its taste, the river that does not know its flow and the mountain that does not know its size, will be made known and heard through me.

And then I pray as I walk through daily life. My prayer is silent and is made of one word: the Name of the Beloved. It is a simple act of remembrance. I breathe in and out His name with each and every breath. Wherever and whenever, while cooking, driving, writing...

But even though this prayer is just one word, for me it includes a larger prayer:

That I see God's face wheresoever I turn,

That I hear His voice in every sound,

That I may serve Him in whatever I do

And that I forget myself so that I can remember Him.

Sometimes I discover that I've forgotten my prayer, and then I give thanks for having been reminded.

There is nothing more important than living prayer without ceasing. Whether I am walking the dog, or gardening, or working with a client, or writing a book, or processing an unresolved emotional place—all these spaces are prayer without ceasing. I am spending my life integrating the idea that my life itself, in all its many phases, is the prayer.

There is a lovely Rumi quote that has been on my mind for days:

I am through with everything but You
Dying into the mystery
I open to Your majesty as an orchard welcomes rain ...

That I am through with everything but You, my beloved—has been true for me, on a soul level, this whole lifetime. Soul knows and lives from that inner knowing that all that matters is my connection with the Divine. Truly. While there are certainly times every day that my personality or my mind has another idea, my soul continues to murmur its truth—that I am through with everything but You.

When my personality and my mind are deeply engaged in demanding that things turn out my way—even though in every request I have ever made of the Universe, I always say, "If this or something better can now be manifested for the greatest good of all concerned"—my mind doesn't really mean that. What I really mean is, "I know what's best for me and the sooner You, my idea of God in the moment, give me that, the better off we will all be." Yet, a still, small voice that's almost like a whisper is always still operating in the background, saying, "I am through with everything but You."

That sweet voice really does have a large sense of acceptance that whatever is going on in my life and business is right for my soul.

I want to remember here, even the moments when I am shouting at God are part of my prayer and part of my intimate relationship with God. God, for me, includes the whole package: my heartbreaking humanity and my awesome connection with the Divine.

How I pray is all day long with all my heart and in all aspects of my life.

I sometimes wonder who first taught me to put my hands in the gesture of prayer. I have a grainy image stored in memory, like an old sepia-colored film, of someone with gray hair tenderly taking my chubby, childish hands and joining them over my heart.

Was it the reverend at my Anglican christening in Hartford? In revisiting this memory I imagine the untold number of people around the world who are, in this very moment, folding their hands over their hearts into this timeless and universal gesture of reverence and remembering. It is a gesture that spans continents and unites Eastern and Western sacred traditions. Somehow prayer and remembering always involves the heart—and finding our heart.

I love when a prayer/poem arrives spontaneously and mysteriously. The exhilarating occasion when an animating force in the heart ignites—perhaps from a moment of "breathing in the world" or from a revelation from within—and the words arrive, tumbling like a current in a river or rise up like foam at high tide.

The poem/prayer I would like to share with you made such a mysterious and ecstatic arrival at the end of a wilderness rites of passage journey with sixteen women on Lama Mountain in New Mexico. I was in the lead as we raced for our destination in front of another approaching storm. We had been "out" for eight days and were exuberant as we saw the fence that marked the gate that meant we were almost home.

This Shining World
A Poem/Prayer of Praise and Gratitude

The boundaries between us
Disappear more each day
No longer solid
Wind blows through me

colleen kelley

I left parts of me on the mountain
Look for me amongst
The leaves and lichen

This shining world
Take off the veils and see
This shining world

I suppose I've never thought about God in my life and never really prayed.

As a doctor, when I'm with someone suffering, if they have a faith, I pray to their faith. I've seen its great power. I take what I find holy—friendship and care—and it comes out in the language of their faith.

The world mirrors the heart. When I was little, I liked to accompany my master, Xiao Yao, when he occasionally visited other monasteries on official business or to see old friends, which could last for days or sometimes even weeks. All the places we visited had a temple similar to ours at Jiuyi Temple, and that was always the first place my Master visited when we arrived.

Xiao Yao would go through the same routine each time inside the temple. First, he would walk up to one of the Buddha statues, meditate in front of it for a while, and then work his way around the room, spending a few moments with all the other statues. Some temples had hundreds of statues. If we were pressed for time, he would pause for only a few seconds in front of each one. But if we had more time, he would close his eyes with his hands in prayer position and remain in a deep meditative state for a long while.

I would mimic him for a few minutes. Then I would grow bored and run off to explore the temple grounds and talk to the monks. When I returned hours later, my Master would still be standing in front of a statue, lost in deep concentration. I once asked Xiao Yao about why he did that, and he replied by retelling the popular story about Master Foyin and the crafty scholar Su Dongpo.

Su Dongpo prided himself on his wit and liked to debate Master Foyin. One day, over tea, he challenged the Master. "Foyin, people think you are an enlightened monk, but to me you just look like a big, stinking pile of worthless dung sitting on your pillow all day long."

Su Dongpo leaned backward and crossed his arms slyly.

Master Foyin placed his hands in prayer position. "My dear Dongpo, but to me you look like a Buddha."

Su Dongpo grinned and bid Master Foyin farewell.

When Su Dongpo got home, he was wearing a triumphant smile. His sister asked him what happened.

"Today I outsmarted Master Foyin," Su Dongpo replied, then recounted the events to her.

"Oh no, brother! I'm sorry to tell you this, but you lost badly," she said.

"What do you mean?"

"Don't you realize that the world mirrors the heart? Master Foyin sees you as a Buddha because he is a Buddha. You see him as a pile of dung. What does that make you?"

Su Dongpo turned beet red, then all of a sudden, he became enlightened.

Xiao Yao elaborated by explaining that he used his "temple rounds" to open his heart to each Buddha statue and merge with it. Going around the room while holding that attitude trained him to become more like Master Foyin, who experienced all people—including a mischief-maker like Su Dongpo—as the living Buddha.

I tell this story each time before I teach one of my favorite practices, *Lotus Meditation*, as it yields the same spiritual benefit that Xiao Yao derived from his temple rounds. But instead of meditating in front of a tangible statue and merging with it, visualize a Holy Being of love of your own choosing, guide it to your heart, and merge with it there. And then as you look around, you'll see *all* the faces before you reflecting back beautiful Buddha smiles.

I aspire to make of my life a prayer—to be awake to the miracle of being. A friend said, as he was dying of cancer, "Every breath without pain is exquisite." That statement often comes to mind and challenges and inspires me to live with radical appreciation for the gift of being alive.

I see feelings of gratitude and love and joy as a form of prayer and have found a way to access these feelings each day. My practice is drawn from many spiritual teachings, such as metta or loving kindness, Vipassana, Chi Gung, guided meditation, Reiki, biofeedback and the Emergence Process.

It is like having a secret lover. I think of myself as a horizontal mystic: I meditate lying down, early in the morning while still in bed. Upon first waking, which is usually an hour before I have to get up, I begin my practice by placing a hand on my heart and one on my belly, sensing their warmth. I focus my awareness on my breath, breathing deeply and slowly.

As suggested by the Institute of Heartmath, I imagine I am breathing in and out through the area of my heart. I access feelings of love and appreciation either by remembering or imagining a time when I experienced them, or simply by invoking the felt sense of these positive emotions.

Even if there is some heaviness of heart, from an anxious dream or a difficult situation in my life, after some time of breathing in and out these good feelings, my heart begins to expand and fill with light. It's as if I am turning on an inner emotional rheostat, intensifying the energy and warmth of positive emotions.

I invoke the full presence of my Higher Self or Essential Self, which is radiant, loving, wise and compassionate. I shift my identity from the separated ego of my personality and become one with this luminous being. My whole being is infused with the radiant, loving energy of essence. I experience soft body bliss. I feel I am resting in a vast field of love, breathing and being breathed by love. I become the Beloved I have been seeking.

From this state of consciousness, I can access guidance and greater wisdom about my life. If I am facing a problem, often a solution or new perspective will arise or the problem seems to dissolve. I set intentions for the day and imagine myself doing what I need to do with the loving energy of my Essential Self. I send blessings to those I love and out into the world.

Indeed, as my friend said as he was close to dying, "Every breath without pain is exquisite." This is the way I pray.

Before explaining exactly how I pray, I want to start by saying that I experience myself to be something like a spectrum. There is really no thing called "me," but more of a spectrum of me, a range of me.

At one end of this spectrum, it is solid: a person, with likes and dislikes and opinions.

At the other end of the spectrum of me there is nothing, *no thing*, just emptiness, spaciousness.

Both can seem to be compelling and exclusively real at times.

In a moment of radical awakening, the spaciousness is completely real and the separate entity called "me" appears unreal. From that perspective, that is the absolute truth of the matter. When you are caught in the identity of "me," on the other hand, then spaciousness has disappeared, and there is only solidity.

When it comes to prayer, I have noticed that we often tend to polarize at one end or the other of this spectrum. If we are caught in the solid "me" end of the spectrum, then there is just "me" and God is completely separate. Then we need to pray to God, and beg to God, and maybe even manipulate God, because God seems very far away. When we are immersed in the feeling of "no me," then prayer seems to be ridiculous. Then we might ask ourselves, "Who is there to pray to, anyway? Who is praying?" The ultimate reality is that there is no separation, and so prayer is just ignorance.

As long as we are in human bodies, we dance, as this spectrum between "me" and "not me" and the entire spectrum is potentially real.

Prayer is actually a function of meditation for me. Prayer and meditation are not separate. Prayer is a flavor of meditation. Sometimes I sit, and I am silent. Spaciousness is there, and thoughts are there, but the spaciousness is quite cool. It is empty, vast and still. There is not so much love in it. If you sit as this spaciousness and wait for a while, you may start to feel that this silent presence becomes warmer. Just through sitting, it starts to warm up, it gets more alive, and it becomes more benevolent.

Now a situation develops which does not make any logical sense. You discover that you are this spaciousness, this presence, at the same time as you are longing passionately for the spaciousness. You are a spectrum, you are not a solid thing, so you are calling out in longing in the same moment that you are being that which is longed for. You are both wave and ocean at the same time.

This is how I would express prayer. It is the full spectrum between calling out in longing for the Beloved, at the same time as resting as the Beloved. The separate dimension of you is saying to the non-separate dimension, "Take me." It is like a raindrop talking to the ocean. They are both water. The raindrop is saying, "Take me. Take me into yourself so completely that I become you and I am not separate from you in any way. Take me over. Embrace me. Let me become so drunk with you that I become you."

chaos, order, secret writing, allyson grey, 2006, oil on board,
23" x 13"

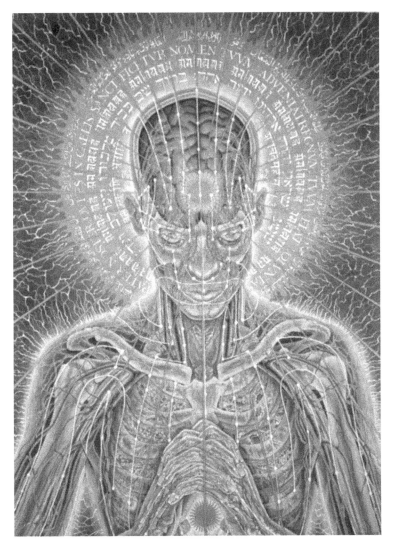

praying, alex grey, 1984, oil on linen, 36" x 48"

Let me share a bit of how I pray.

I begin with my body, allowing it to find a comfortable pace as I walk from my house to the trail that runs beside Lytle Creek about a mile from my home. As my body finds its stride, it prays wordlessly with every step, and as this walking prayer engulfs my body from heel to head, my body prayer opens into heart song and I chant aloud in Hebrew, English and Sanskrit, singing the names of God as I follow the creek until it flows into Stones River.

Not long after I have reached Stones River, the chanting aloud stops and I find myself suddenly and effortlessly in conversation with the Divine Mother—God—as I encounter God in my daily practice. For me, She is *Chochma/Sophia*, the Wisdom of the Ineffable manifest in, with, as and through the universe. She is the Ocean and the Wave, but not yet the wetness of both. She is the doorway to the Ineffable, who incarnates as all life and is most fully present in those rare lives that allow Her to manifest most powerfully: Jesus, Krishna, Buddha, Rumi, etc.

My conversation with the Mother begins with thanksgiving. I am grateful for whatever is—both good and bad, success and failure. I don't believe She has a plan for my life that I can beg Her to reveal, nor do I believe She is open to changing what is to accommodate what I might want to be. She is what is, and what is must be, given the conditions of the moment, and this opening conversation is simply an experience of radical acceptance.

From gratitude I move to self-reflection, with the Divine Mother mirroring back to me the quality of my actions, stripped bare of the rationalizations in which I seek to clothe them. I see the suffering I cause, and am moved to makes amends and do differently. I hear the insanity that passes for normalcy in my life, and drop it as one might drop a hot coal. (True, I pick it up again as soon as it cools to the touch, but that is why this is an ongoing process.)

This conversation is dialogical and still quite egoic: there is a clear "I" speaking at this point, reviewing the day gone by and imagining and setting intentions for the day now unfolding. I have no delusion that the Mother is the Absolute. She is merely that of God which I can encounter, given who am I today.

While this conversation can be rich, it is often short: as my body is still walking, and my heart is still chanting, my mind can't maintain for long its cherished sense of separateness. Soon the mind fades into soul, and I begin to see Her as everything. There is still an "I" in this process, though not the same "I" as in the conversation. Every tree, every squirrel, rabbit, deer and dog I meet is suddenly the Mother. Even the people I meet are Her, and when I say "hello," I cannot help but know I am saying hello to Her and She to me.

This is often the longest stretch of my four-mile prayer, and as I return to my house and enter my home it is often filled with Her presence. I remove my shoes and settle into my meditation corner to sit. As body opened heart, and both opened mind and then soul, now there is the possibility that soul will ripen into spirit. I have done all I can do, the rest is a matter of Divine Grace. If it happens, good. If not, also good. It has nothing to do with me. And when it happens, it has even less to do with me, for "I" am gone.

With the ripening of spirit, self and other drop away. There is no "Rami," no "Mother," no "this" or "that." The ocean and wave are simply wetness. There may be a subject but there is no object. There may be awareness, but there is nothing of which to be aware. So of this I must be silent for I have never experienced it.

What I have experienced is the aftermath of the ripening spirit. Reb Nachman of Breslav, a 19th-century Hasidic sage, has a word for this: *rishimu*. Imagine buying a bottle of expensive perfume and leaving it open on a table. In time, the oil will evaporate until there is nothing left of the perfume except its fragrance now permeating the entire room. This is *rishimu*.

As spirit reemerges as soul, mind, heart and body there is a fragrance that permeates all these dimensions. It is the perfume of compassion. And while it lasts I feel love for and from all things. For me, it doesn't last long enough, but again, this is not a once-and-for-all prayer, but a once-and-once-again process. So I make a closing vow to link my thoughts, feelings, words and deeds in service to justice and compassion, and I get up to go about my day.

How do I pray? I close my eyes and clasp my hands in front of my heart. I feel the warmth that fills my heart as soon as I do this. There's immediate Presence.

Sometimes I pray for something, usually the greatest good in any given situation. Or I ask for guidance. Or with trust, I turn over a situation to God, the Light, the Great Mother, the Great Spirit, the Christ, whatever name arises in the moment. Or I just communicate with that Presence, beyond words and names, its peace, wholeness, healing and love.

I open my eyes, light is everywhere and I am in that radiant Presence. Prayer is a reminder that we live always in a state of grace.

When we do a group prayer, we first intone the note of 528 Hertz. This idea was originally taught by Dr. Len Halbit in Hawaii. According to his theory, this is the basic frequency of the universe. The reason we use this frequency is that in our physical realm, it is very difficult to connect with the universe. We need to send our prayer to the universe and then through the universe, via this frequency.

After we intone 528 Hertz, the frequency for transformation and DNA repair, we chant the Grand Invocation—a world prayer translated into fifty languages and dialects—so the power and spirit of words can be activated. Usually, people chant the invocation in Japanese, but the meaning of these words is that the eternal power of the universe can be crystallized and true harmony can be received in the world. We chant this mantra three times.

Afterwards, we say four phrases to send our thanks, love and apologies to the water, and seek forgiveness from the water. We say, "Water, we are sorry; water, please forgive us; water, we love you and water, we thank you." We then close our eyes and offer a quiet prayer for one minute. In this prayer, usually we visualize the spirit of water and send our prayer to that spirit. Often, we also offer a song to the water. Usually, I choose a piece from Beethoven's Symphony No. 9, "Ode to Joy." This is the sequence of my prayer.

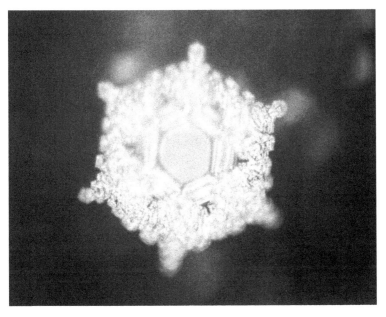

love and gratitude water crystal © office masaru emoto, llc

gail straub

Prayer, walking and landscape are inextricably related for me. I pray daily during an hour-long walk near my home in the Catskill Mountains along the Ashokan Reservoir. In the native Esopus language, Ashokan means "the place of many fishes." Indeed, it feels auspicious to pray in this place of many fishes. The bluestone and shale mountain guardians—Balsam Cap, Slide, Table, Wittenburg, Indian Head and Overlook—form a protective bowl around the Ashokan. Walking a path right along the reservoir, I am often blessed by eagles, red-tailed hawks, wild geese or blue heron. My ritual is to say a round of my own prayers, followed by my version of the Rosary and the Hail Mary for particular people or issues.

First are prayers for my husband David and myself.

Hail Mary,
Full of Grace....

Then are prayers for family and dear friends.

The Lord is with thee...

Prayers for my students or those in need,

Blessed art thou among women,
and blessed is the fruit
of thy womb, Jesus.

Prayers for the Obama family,

Holy Mary,
Mother of God...

And prayers for the world.

Pray for us now,
and at the hour of death.
Amen.

All the while, as I am walking and praying, the landscape is also praying with me as well as in me. In the winter, snow can suddenly blow in, leaving a soft, quiet, white blanket, a feeling of space and emptiness. "Remember to empty out," the land is saying, "remember that quiet space is an interior quality always available to you."

As spring harkens, the red buds form a pink haze like a delicate woven shawl warming the mountain range. The mother eagle sits patiently on her nest and wild geese parade with their ducklings as the Earth announces the miracle of rebirth that follows every winter. I am reminded to pay attention to the death and rebirth inside me.

Summer walks witness wild thunderstorms clapping across the sky, followed, on rare days, by unexpected rainbows arching across the Ashokan. The storms' sight, sound and smell invite the bold, the sensual, and the passionate aspects of praying.

Then, as I walk at the peak of autumn's orange, red, rust and yellow splendor, a dense fog might roll in. Suddenly the colors have vanished, and yet I know that they are still there, bright as ever. This is the landscape's gentle invitation to faith, to trust that my prayers burn brilliant even when I cannot see the evidence of this.

Walking, praying—through the landscape's seasons, through the seasons of my life.

Recalling the places where the Earth is unstable, in danger, out of balance in any way, and where the need for healing is very great, we send our love and caring to relieve the suffering of the Earth. Resting in the awareness of the vast, interconnected web of life, we form the intention that this Earth Treasure Vase, filled with sacred offerings from our heart of hearts, once buried in the Earth, will radiate healing and protective energies out in every direction for all time, and that the healing be accomplished, the vitality of the Earth restored.

earth treasure vase, held by cynthia jurs, founder of the earth treasure vase global healing project, santa fe, new mexico.
photo © jennifer esperanza

As a Buddhist, I do not engage in petitionary prayer, but use a practice that combines devotion, aspiration and meditation.

I begin my session with the act of "going for refuge," turning to the "Three Jewels" as my guides and sources of consolation. I take refuge in the Buddha as the supreme teacher, and wish that all sentient beings understand the ultimate truth and arouse the unsurpassed aspiration. I take refuge in the Dharma, the Buddha's teaching, the law of righteousness and truth, and wish that all sentient beings enter deeply into the truth, with wisdom as deep as the ocean. I take refuge in the Sangha, the community of realized disciples, and wish that all sentient beings come together in harmony, without obstruction.

I then remind myself that the quest for enlightenment is the core of my life, the value that takes priority over all others. But to ensure that this quest does not turn into a private project, I also recollect that I seek enlightenment, not for myself alone, but in order to bring benefit and happiness to countless others.

To keep my priorities in order, I then briefly reflect on death. This is done by calling to mind three facts: death is inevitable and inescapable; the arrival of death is uncertain and may even occur this very day; and when I die I must relinquish everything, not only external possessions, but even my body and personal identity.

I then briefly generate the four immeasurable attitudes: loving-kindness, the wish that all beings be well and happy; compassion, the wish that all who suffer be free from suffering; altruistic joy, the joy that arises by rejoicing in the merits and virtues of others; and equanimity, the ability to look upon all beings with impartiality.

Following this, I focus my mind on a mental image of the Buddha. I see the Buddha as the visible manifestation of perfect purity, wisdom and compassion. For about ten minutes I visualize the Buddha's image as best I can, radiant and sublime, full of goodness and grace. This helps the mind to settle down.

When the mind has settled, I direct my awareness to the body, experiencing the body as a whole, keeping in mind simply the felt sensations of the body in the sitting posture. I let my awareness extend over the whole body and note bodily sensations as they arise and pass away. If sensations become especially intense in a particular area, I direct my attention there, again focusing on the flow of bodily sensations. If those intense sensations subside, I return my attention to the body in its wholeness. Sometimes, to strengthen concentration, I deliberately focus on a specific area. At other times, I apply a panoramic awareness that picks up the felt sense of body as an organic totality. If my thoughts become scattered, I might again conjure up the image of the Buddha and focus on it for a few minutes before returning to the stream of bodily sensations.

Awareness of the constant arising and passing of bodily sensations highlights, at a microscopic level, the principle of *anicca*, impermanence, the fact that everything that comes into being passes away. And since the body and all its sensations are impermanent, I can see that they are not a self, but only a selfless, insubstantial process, devoid of an inner core. This is the principle of *anatta*, non-self.

When my meditation session comes to an end, usually after fifty minutes, I conclude the session by sharing the merits of my practice. I briefly call to mind those beings that have already reached high attainments and rejoice in their merits and virtues. Then I share the merits of my own practice with all beings throughout the universe, wishing them to be well and happy and free from suffering.

The most intensely intimate period of prayer in my life came when I was caring for my mother who was ill with multiple myeloma cancer and eventually died. All the years of practice—silent meditation, repetition of the holy name, one-pointed attention—came rushing in, providing support during this time of insurmountable grief that was blanketed in profound awe and reverence.

"God's will be done." I continually repeated in the depths of my heart. Simultaneously, every cell of my being cried out, *"Please, dear God, do not take her from me."*

Clutching mala beads, I repeated my mantra constantly—sometimes silently, other times chanting softly—as I sat for nearly two weeks by my mother's bedside. Praying to God was the only open channel available to stay connected to her as a terminal coma set in due to her kidney failure.

No longer could I relate with my mother's outer form. She was leaving this world and I had to surrender to what was happening. Every moment became a prayer as I clung to the One who gives life and who was now removing life from her body.

It was all happening so quickly, like sand slipping through an hourglass. I prayed for her protection, inwardly and outwardly. I prayed that she have no suffering.

Infused with the grace of love, I felt the veil between this world and the next thin and lift momentarily. I prayed that, as she left her body and this worldly realm of my gentle touch, she would be greeted and held by loving souls—family and friends who had passed on before her.

How incredibly painful this was! How immensely beautiful! Letting go of my beloved one to the Beloved One. My chest was physically sore from the heartache of losing her. I longed to be united fully with God, as she soon would be.

"Follow the Buddha," I whispered in her ear just moments before she passed. "Follow Kwan Yin. Our love will carry you on your journey." Exhaling her final breath, a profound silence enveloped us and an invisible portal opened to another realm.

I continue to pray every day for my mother. Silently, I bring her image into my heart center and send her love. May she be safe, protected and happy wherever her soul's journey takes her.

I pray to the birds because I believe they will carry the messages
  of my heart upward.
I pray to them because I believe in their existence,
   the way their songs begin and end each day—the invocations
   and benedictions of Earth.
I pray to the birds because they remind me of what I love rather
  than what I fear.
And at the end of my prayers, they teach me how to listen.

Westerners are suspicious of prostrations, which smacks to them of idol worship. But from the Chan (Chinese Zen) perspective, prostration is an art, a highly developed spiritual technology.

In the center of my palm is a space, which represents emptiness. Everything is created in the here and now, and emptiness is the true nature of our hearts and minds. As I stand to begin my prostration, I have the awareness that what is here and now is only a state of mind, and whatever it is can change. I can change it.

I bow and make a *mudra* by the wrapping the palm of my left hand over the fist of the right; my two index fingers come up to touch each other. The shape of my hands represents the lotus bud, the lotus bloom in Buddhism that symbolizes the beautiful, fragrant flower of wisdom and compassion—Buddhahood—that grows out of the mud of *samsara*, the endless cycle of death, rebirth and suffering to which the material world is bound.

I bow to signify humility, the humble, transforming the mind. I am a bud, a Buddha to be.

I bring my hand up to the level of my eyes. My eyes see the bud. It represents offering, generosity, respect. The bud is my heart and I offer it to all sentient beings. I clasp my palms again and prostrate to the ground. My hands and arms are out in front of me. I touch the earth like a lightning rod, grounding myself.

This part of the prostration is what may be particularly unseemly to some Westerners. The supine posture of prostration represents renunciation. I let go of the ego, of arrogance and pride, the cause of so many of our problems. I turn my open palms upward. They are my heart and mind. I turn them upward to receive wisdom and compassion. I close my palms to bring the wisdom and compassion into my heart and mind. I turn my palms around to touch the earth with all its dirt and muck, all those things we suppress, that we don't want to face, that we sweep under the carpet. In Buddhism, we transform by facing the dirt, by touching it. We touch it with wisdom and compassion.

As I slowly stand, I am the lotus coming up out of the muck, out of the dirt, starting again, fresh and new. I have transformed my heart and mind. I have transformed troubled relationships and this troubled world.

In prostrations, I touch the sick, the suffering, those who are lost in grief, frustration and despair. I touch the dying. I connect all of life with humility, generosity and respect. I touch the great Earth.

How does a secular neuroscience researcher pray? By looking at the overwhelming evidence showing that any form of positive, intensive contemplative activity imparts benefits to one's physical, emotional and cognitive health. Buddhist meditation, Hindu yoga, Christian centering prayers, Sufi chanting, self-hypnosis, deep relaxation, positive affirmations, mantras, mudras, mindful eating and moment-to-moment observations of our inner feelings, thoughts and sensations all have the power to change the structure and function of the brain in ways that lower stress, anxiety, depression, anger and blood pressure. They enhance memory, concentration, social awareness, compassion, empathy and moral decision-making. And it doesn't matter if you're a believer, agnostic or nonbeliever.

So how do I pray? By combining as many practices as I can throughout the day, and creating my own. I'll wake up and go to sleep with a brief forgiveness, gratitude, and loving kindness meditation. I'll do Islamic prayers with my Sufi wife several times a day. I'll eat my meals and exercise with mindfulness. I'll observe my feelings and thoughts when I'm angry or sad, without judgment. I'll practice compassionate communication when I speak and listen to others. I'll translate ancient Jewish and Christian poetry, immersing myself in the sacred texts of the world. And I'll yawn, because the evidence shows that this is the fastest way to generate relaxation, attentiveness and increased consciousness throughout the brain.

ganga white

What If?

What if our religion was each other?
If our practice was our life?
If prayer was our words?
What if the Temple was the Earth?
If forests were our church?
If holy water—the rivers, lakes and oceans?
What if meditation was our relationships?
If the Teacher was life?
If wisdom was self-knowledge?
If love was the center of our being?

The first practice that is really important to me is Conversational Prayer. Brother Lawrence, a seventeenth-century Carmelite monk, encouraged people to simply talk to God every day as they go through the tasks of their day. The Hasidic master Rebbe Nachman of Breslov said, "Talk to God as you would talk to your very best friend. Tell The Holy One everything." And so I follow their advice. I try to begin my meditations with a conversation with God. I try to open every single corner of my heart and life to God. I try to invite God in, so all can be seen, acknowledged and related to this all-accepting and reassuring presence that I feel as a result. I speak of my joys, my struggles and at times of special difficulties I just sit there and cry until there are no more tears to shed. Sometimes I also invite some of the saints that I feel close to. I talk to them, I cry with them, and I rejoice with them. This practice usually leads to a receptive silence in which I can simply say yes to God and what may be, where I can let go of my ideas about what's right and simply surrender to God's will.

I sat next to my grandfather during my youth on the hard pews of the Christian church we attended. The warm tears in his eyes as he looked down at me at his side told me everything about God. And it is to this loving God that I pray.

Prayer for me is gratitude. "Thank you, thank you, thank you, God/Goddess" is standard basic prayer, and then it gets more detailed from there. I seldom "ask" for anything, but I do affirm the positive result I am seeking. In other words, I thank God for all I receive long before it actually happens. I spend a good deal of time communicating with the divine! The divine for me is in everything.

Remembering to pray as a formality is harder than defining *how* I pray as a moment-by-moment event. And so I affirm that every action is a prayer, every interaction is prayer and every word I speak in communicating with others and with myself is a dialogue with the divine. In fact, I often observe people observing me as I go about my life in conversation with an invisible companion. People will ask "Are you talking to yourself?" and I wonder about this. Perhaps I am in a constant state of prayer with my own divine self, now that you ask! They also comment that I seem to be having a *wonderful* time with my invisible companion and I assure these curiosity seekers that I am usually in a natural state of bliss or joy.

I believe this comes from maintaining a consistent dialogue with creation and all that She provides. I do pray to Her as well as Him, even though I know "they" are not *hims* or *hers*... but *all*.

If by prayer, we mean, "Please, God, give me a pony," I don't do that. I don't see a "God" that is sitting down at some quantum computer saying, "Oh, Sharif wants a pony, let's give him one." If "prayer" means petitioning a transcendent being and getting stuff, then I don't pray.

However, I *am* in a near constant conversation with the Divine. Aspects of that conversation are formal. In the morning, I sit down and I light candles. I light a stick of incense. I sit in a particular seat in a particular way. I set a timer, I close my eyes, and I then engage in a conversation that does not have words, that's outside of this space, this time, this being.

At one point in time in my life I thought you had to wear certain kinds of clothes, go to a particular building and do particular gestures in a particular way—that was "praying." That might be praying, but there's a really good chance that it is just a habitual cultural exercise.

Rocks are sacred, stars are sacred, trees are sacred, rivers are sacred. How could you harm the Earth if you are a PART of the Earth? This is the kind of sacredness indigenous people have always known, and to which we must return.

ALL beings have consciousness. *All of them*. The Sun is a living being. It breathes, over an eleven-year cycle. Scientists look at it as a thermonuclear process, but we can choose to look at it as our Father. Scientists look at this Earth as various dynamic geological and hydrodynamic processes, but we can choose to look at it as our Mother.

These are not quaint truisms—this is reality. Reality is that all LIFE is conscious. Everything, even what we call "inanimate" objects, is alive. Other beings just have a consciousness that we don't yet understand. Just because we don't understand it, doesn't mean it's not there.

And so our challenge is to let go of the notion that WE represent the standard of both "life" and "consciousness." We must get to the point where we are engaged in a constant conversation with the All, where we can see the All in all settings.

We have to stop looking for "life" or "consciousness" or "God" in a particular church or temple. We have to start recognizing that consciousness is EVERYWHERE.

So this relationship to the Source that I call "prayer" brings us full circle. How do I pray? I pray by paying attention—with my full consciousness. I think that's all we can do. Pay attention—open our heart and pay attention.

gloria karpinski

I Am A Being of Light,
Daughter/Son of the Mother-Father-God
This day only that which is for my Highest Good shall come to me.
Only that which is Light shall leave from me.
Thank you Mother-Father-God.

I am an atheist. This may not seem to particularly qualify me to talk about spiritual matters. But I believe it does, and uniquely: I see atheism as a sort of minimalist spiritual perspective, one that has stripped away so much of what we usually *think* of as spiritual—the supernatural—that the *essence* of spirituality can be seen more clearly.

People will ask me: *Don't you believe in God?* No, I don't. *Jesus? Buddha?* I believe that both were men of great charisma and insight—but neither was a god. *Don't you believe in anything?* Of course I do.

I believe in two things above all: Nature and love. Nature is all-powerful. Love is how I understand the good. It might have been nice to believe in God, often defined as all-powerful *and* good, but combining the two like that has always posed too much of a contradiction for my poor mind to believe in.

It's the old problem of evil: If he's all-powerful and all-loving, why does he then permit evil? If you want to get specific, why does he allow innocent children to suffer (and they do suffer, don't they?). Me, I have nature—which I hold in great esteem, but which is clearly not loving—and love—which is good, but clearly not all-powerful.

What about an afterlife? No, I don't believe in that either. *You mean you think we just die and that's it?* Yes, that's right. *So how can you stand to live?* Life is enough. It has to be—it's all there is. *But then what's the meaning of life?* The meaning of life is in the living of it.

Our lives are such small things. Sometimes we think we need something grand to make them worthwhile—like eternal life in paradise, or great success, or intense experiences. Or we feel we need a grand philosophy or religion to give our lives meaning. But that's just not true.

It's the little moments of happiness in life that give it meaning: Some laughter; some conversation; good food; a little sex; satisfaction at a job well done; a walk on the beach; making a difference, even if it's a small difference; seeing your children become happy, healthy, productive adults; washing your car; a game of cards; a good movie; a beer ... God (if you'll pardon the expression) is in the details.

So just lie back and enjoy life—sounds pretty hedonistic! Perhaps, if your idea of hedonism includes doing your best and loving others. *Then what's the difference between an ordinary life and meaningful life?* Attitude!

The world is so incredibly rich, so incredibly complex, that it can overwhelm us. We retreat from the richness of life and love into the semi-conscious state of the workaday world. We retreat into roles and rituals and habits and defensiveness and alcohol and television ... We sleepwalk through life, and miss the good stuff.

And life is hard. *Very* hard for many people. Nature is what it is, does what it does, whether we enjoy it or not. And people, while capable of love, often don't show it. So we close our eyes and hearts to protect ourselves. Perhaps we even grow a thick layer of callus over our innermost selves. But if we close our eyes and hearts, again we miss the good stuff.

This is why we need to face our problems instead of hiding from them, accept anxiety and sadness and even pain as inevitable parts of life, rather than pretending that we can only be happy when life is perfect. If we shut down when unhappiness comes our way, we may not feel as much pain, but we are no longer open to the small, good things of life that make it meaningful.

So we just have to buck up and deal? In a way, it does all come down to that. *You can't do it alone—you need God's help!* That would be nice—but that kind of help doesn't seem forthcoming! *It seems like you are asking a lot of a people all by themselves.* But we *aren't* all by ourselves.

We aren't as alone as we think we are, each of us locked away in some soul-walnut. I believe that consciousness is only occasionally restricted to one person's mind. Most of the time, it lies somewhere between us.

If you are playing pool with a friend, and you are really concentrating on the game, for a little while the two of you are actually sharing consciousness—he sees what you see and you see what he sees. When you make love with someone, you become lost in each other, lost in the passion of the moment, and share consciousness. When you raise your children, you pass on your values and dreams and quirks, and every now and then they will see the world through your eyes, and you through theirs. I'm not talking about ESP or psychic phenomena here. I'm just suggesting that we never lived in such separate egos in the first place. We all learn to *believe* we are isolated, but we aren't.

That's how love works: To love means to realize that you and the other person aren't entirely separate, that his or her needs and feelings are yours. It is looking in someone's eyes and seeing yourself. And that provides us with one more source of meaning!

Okay. So you have some meaning in your life. But you don't have ultimate meaning, do you? No.

Ultimately, as far as nature is concerned, my poor atheist philosophy says it makes no difference if we shut out both good and bad or experience both good and bad fully—six of one, half a dozen of the other. Love, or don't love? It doesn't matter to nature. But with open eyes and hearts we do find meaning, even if it isn't glorified with the title of "ultimate."

I have no desire to convert anyone to atheism. It seems rather absurd to try to convert someone to nothing! But I do think that, even if we put away our various and complex religious belief systems, the possibility for a fulfilling life remains. Perhaps the possibility is even enhanced.

At this very moment all prayers are already answered. There are no wants necessary, no needs, no *shoulds* or *shouldn'ts*, so of course we are perfectly fulfilled, though we may not know it. Prayers can only be answered in the moment. Nothing else is necessary; nothing else is possible or ever has been or ever will be. That's where we always are. And how wonderful the moment is when the mind finally becomes still enough to recognize that!

Prayer evokes that power within us that is capable of everything. But when we pray *for* something, it is always the story of the past projected as the future. No prayer changes the past. We don't get a vote about what is. What *is* is. Prayers don't change what happened. *Seeing* the past differently—questioning our thoughts about the past—is what changes it, right here, right now, and prayer can work that way also.

I often say that if I had a prayer, it would be this: *God, spare me from the desire for love, approval or appreciation. Amen.* I don't have a prayer, in fact, because I don't want anything but what I have. I know the benevolence of life. Why would I pray for something different, which would always be less than what comes? God is another name for reality. It's complete, it's perfect, it fills me with the utmost joy. The thought of asking for what isn't never even arises.

But if I still believed my thoughts, I would pray for one thing first: to be spared from the desire for love. This desire causes nothing but confusion and misery. It shuts down the awareness of what you already have in reality. It's painful to seek what you can never have outside yourself. I say "can never have" because obviously you don't understand what you're seeking. If you understood it, the seeking would be over. Because you think you know what love looks like, what it should or shouldn't be, it becomes invisible to you. It's the blind seeking what doesn't exist. You beg, you plead, you bend over backward and do all sorts of other emotional acrobatics in this unending search for happy endings. Only by seeking the truth within will you find the love you can never lose. And when you find it, your natural response is gratitude.

71

This would be my one prayer, because the answer to it brings the end of time and space. It brings the energy of pure, unlimited mind, set free in all its power and goodness. When you stop seeking love, it leaves you with nothing to do; it leaves you with the experience of being "done" in a doing that is beyond you. It's absolutely effortless. And a whole lot gets done in it, beyond what you think could ever have been accomplished.

When I don't look for approval outside me, I remain as approval. And through inquiry I have come to see that I want you to approve of what you approve of, because I love you. What you approve of is what I want. That's love—it wouldn't change anything. It already has everything it wants. It already *is* everything it wants, just the way it wants it.

Living fearlessly is natural when you've questioned your thoughts. People ask me what that looks like today, and in answer, I sometimes tell the story of the birth of my granddaughter Marley. When Roxann, my daughter, went into labor, we were all there in the delivery room—me, my husband and my son-in-law Scott and his parents. Everything was going well until suddenly the baby got stuck in the birth canal. She began to sink back into the womb, and her heart went into distress. The hospital was small, and on this night, at three in the morning, it was understaffed. The doctor had no qualified assistant and I noticed a sense of panic in the room. The doctor decided on a caesarean section, brusquely dismissed us and wheeled Roxann into surgery. She was screaming and no one would tell us anything, so we had reasons to believe that she and her baby were in serious trouble. Then the screams stopped. We could hear angry- or panicked-sounding instructions being given at the end of the hall. An assistant from the emergency room ran toward me with a phone number, asked me to call it and tell the person who answered to come to the hospital immediately, then ran off without explaining what it was all about. After I made the call, I walked over to Scott's parents, who are Christians. When they saw me, they said, "Katie, will you pray with us?" The question surprised me. I didn't have a reference for prayer. I looked into their dear, tired, frightened

eyes and thought, *There's nothing I need to ask for. I want whatever God wants.*
But I took their hands, of course. They closed their eyes and prayed and
I stood there with them, loving them, knowing how painful it can be to
want a particular outcome.

During this experience, there was no internal resistance, no fear. For
me, reality is God. I can always trust that. I don't have to guess what God's
will is. Whatever happens is God's will, whether my child and grandchild
live or die, and therefore it's my will. So my prayers are already answered.
I love Roxann with all my heart, and I would gladly have given my life to
save hers, and that was not being called for. As it happened, the caesarean
section went well, and both Roxann and Marley were fine.

There is another way. If I had believed such thoughts as, "It's better
for Roxann to live than to die" or "My granddaughter should be born,"
or "The doctor should have been better prepared," I would have been
very upset. I might have barged into the emergency room, making
it even more difficult for the staff. There might have been anger,
frustration, terror or prayers (the kind that attempt to manipulate
what can never be manipulated). These are a few of the ways we react
when we believe what we think. It's what the war with reality often
looks like, and it's not only insane, it's hopeless and very painful.

But when you question your mind, thoughts flow in and out
and don't cause any stress because you don't believe them. And you
instantly realize that their opposites could be just as true. In that
peace of mind, reality shows you that there are no problems, only
solutions. You know, to your very depths, that whatever happens is
what should be happening. If I lose my grandchild or my daughter, I
lose what wasn't mine in the first place. It's a good thing. Either that,
or God is a sadist—and that's not my experience.

I don't order God around. I don't presume to know whether life
or death is better for me or for anyone I love. How can I know that?
All I know is that God is everything and God is good. That's my
story, and I'm sticking to it.

daniel craig

Creator, thank you for who I am and who I am not. Thank you for
where I am and where I am not. Thank you for what I am and what
I am not. Thank you for everything, and for the nothing—the void
from which I arrived.

core witness prayers for peace, daniel craig, veteran for peace, santa fe, new mexico. photo © jennifer esperanza

I pray in relationship to the sacred Self within as I allow myself to descend there in daily practice. I pray as I settle my back against a scraggy pine tree at ten thousand feet in a Colorado forest—the pine pitch sticking to my back, its odor wafting through the air. "Forgive us our trespasses against you," I whisper to the icy mountain stream, which is clear, transparent, pristine, yet undrinkable because of what the latest horde of campers may have left in it. "Have mercy upon us," I cry to the sandy slopes in January, normally snow-covered, but laid bare by climate chaos.

I pray as I look in the eyes of my dog and see no ego, only unconditional love. On this frigid, frosty night, we snuggle and keep warm. I bless our body heat and the warm shower I was able to take this morning.

I pray for those who cannot eat, who will live on two dollars today if they are lucky. I can't feed you there in the sweltering African desert, but I can pray by feeding your brother or sister here in the homeless shelter that is less than a mile away—and by giving thanks:

"I give you thanks for this incredibly delicious meal—these succulent vegetables, the grain of this bread, the water with which I make tea. I honor and bless all who grew this food, who cut, ground, wrapped and sold it to me. I give thanks that I had the resources with which to purchase it."

And my friend, I pray as I walk with you, listen to you, share my dreams with you, tell you ancient stories with my drum, sit with you in your sorrow, hold your hand or, on another day, allow you to wipe the tears from my eyes.

I bring myself back from mental obsession, future-casting, back-casting and all that is less than everlasting, to this holy, sacred moment. I pray as I return to my relationship with this, now that this is the only reality. And that it is truly enough.

You discover yourself, not in isolation, not in withdrawal, but in relationship... —J. Krishnamurti

I pray not for divine intervention in the world around me, but for divine intervention in my mind, for therein lies the root of my discontent.

We usually think of prayer as an appeal to God, or some other spiritual entity, to change the world in some way. We might pray for someone's healing, for success in some venture, for a better life or for guidance on some challenging issue. Behind such prayers is the recognition that we don't have the power to make the world the way we would like it to be—if we did, we would simply get on with the task—so we beseech a higher power to change things for us.

Changing the world in some way or another occupies much of our time and attention. We want to get the possessions, opportunities or experiences that we think will make us happy—or conversely, avoid those that will make us suffer. We believe that if only things were different we would be happy.

This is the ego's way of thinking. It is founded on the belief that how we feel inside depends upon what is going on around us. When the world is not the way we think it should be, we become discontent. This can take many forms—dissatisfaction, disappointment, frustration, annoyance, irritation, depression, despair, sadness, impatience, intolerance, judgment, grievance, grumbling. Yet whatever form the discontent may take, it is actually a creation of our own minds. It stems from how we see things, from the interpretations we put on our experience.

For example, if I am stuck in a traffic jam, I can see it as something that is going to make me suffer later—being late for an appointment, missing some experience or upsetting someone—and thus begin to feel anxious, frustrated or impatient. Or I can see it as the chance to relax, take it easy and do nothing for a few minutes. Same situation, two totally different reactions. And the difference is purely in my mind.

The ego believes it has my best interests at heart, and holds onto its view of what I need. Locked into a fixed perception like this, it is hard for me to see that I am stuck. I believe the fault lies in the world out there, rather than my beliefs about how things should be. So I tell myself a story of what should change in order for me to be happy, and set about trying to make that happen.

When I find I cannot make the world the way I think it should be, then I might, if the need seems sufficiently important, beseech some higher power to intervene and change things for me. I am, in effect, asking it to do the bidding of my ego. Yet, as most of us have discovered, the ego seldom knows what is truly best for us.

If, on the other hand, I recognize that my suffering may be coming from the way I am seeing things, then it makes more sense to ask, not for a change in the world, but for a change in my thinking. I may pray for the traffic jam to go away, when it might be wiser to pray that my feelings of frustration and tension go away.

The help I need is in stepping out of the ego's way of seeing. So when I pray, I ask, with an attitude of innocent curiosity: "Could there, perhaps, be another way of seeing this?" I do not try to answer the question myself, for that would doubtless activate the ego mind, which loves to try and work things out for me. So I simply pose the question, let it go and wait.

What then often happens is that a new way of seeing dawns on me. It does not come as a verbal answer; it comes as an actual shift in perception. I find myself seeing the situation in a new way.

One of the first times I prayed this way concerned some difficulties that I was having with my partner. She was not behaving the way I thought she should. (And how many of us have not felt that at times?) After a couple of days of strained relationship, I decided to pray, just inquiring if there might possibly be another way of perceiving this.

Almost immediately, I found myself seeing her in a very different light. Here was another human being, with her own history and her own needs, struggling to navigate a difficult situation. Suddenly everything looked different. I felt compassion for her rather than animosity, understanding rather than judgment. I realized that for the last two days I had been out of love; but now the love had returned.

With conventional prayer, I might have prayed for her to change. But the divine intervention I needed was not in her behavior, but in my own mind, in the mindsets that were running my thinking.

The results of praying like this never cease to impress me. Invariably, I find my fears and judgments drop away. In their place is a sense of ease. Whoever or whatever was troubling me, I now see through more loving and compassionate eyes. Moreover, the new way of seeing often seems so obvious: Why hadn't I seen this before? Asking this simple question allows me access to my inner knowing, and lets it shine into my life.

The answer does not always come as rapidly as in the above example. Sometimes the shift happens later—in a dream or when relaxing, doing nothing. The prayer sows the seed; it germinates in its own time. Nor do I always get answers to such prayers. However, even if I only get an answer half the time, those times make the asking well worthwhile.

The beauty of this approach is that I am not praying to some power beyond myself. I am praying to my own self for guidance. Below the surface thinking of my ego-mind, my inner being knows the truth. It sees where I have become caught in a particular mindset, and is ever-willing to help set me free.

jeff sollins

I pray from my Heart
But I listen with my Soul.

My prayers are at once complex and simple. Since beginning a journey through Jewish orthodoxy, my sense of awe toward the mundane has begun to emerge with daily synchronicity.

With humility and wonder, I wish to share a manifestation of the miraculous.

For thirty years I have searched for my *Beshert*—my soul mate—from Baltimore to California to New York to Texas to Florida to New Mexico to Israel. For years I have dreamed, and against the odds of time and space, I have kept my belief that somewhere my special someone was waiting.

In the realm of Chassidic mysticism, there are special prayers—specific portions of Tehillim—psalms by King David—and physical actions known as mitzvot, such as giving charity, which can draw down spiritual blessings.

As you can imagine, however, after so many years I had become a bit dream weary; but never did I give up my hope and trust in Hashem's interest in our lives.

And it was then, as I had almost accepted my fate to go through life as a single man, that I met Rabbi Kamenetski of Dnepropetrosvk, Ukraine at the Lubavitcher Rebbe's *yartziet* in Crown Heights in July 2009. The rabbi asked if I would be interested in speaking to the Jewish community in Dnepr on integrative holistic medicine and added, "By the way, there are many single Jewish women there." He assured me I would be engaged by Chanukah. This was my Mom's *yahrzeit*, the day of her passing, so I smiled inside and said, "I have heard this many times before, but I will come and we shall see."

According to the Bal Shem Tov, the founder of Chassidus, THERE ARE NO COINCIDENCES. Everyone you meet has a message for you if your heart is ready to hear and see and feel.

I landed in Dnepr on 9/8/2009 ... and asked, "What am I doing here?" As I was getting off the plane, the city appeared bleak, dreary and—excuse me—very third world.

And here I will find my *Beshert*?

On 9/9/2009 at 5:00 p.m. I met Maryna, and exactly two Chanukahs later, on December 21, 2011, Kislev 25, 5772—the first day of Chanukah and my mom's *yahrzeit*—we were married.

I pray from my Heart
I listen with my Soul

Prayer is My Heart and Soul.

With Hashem's blessings, we celebrated our second anniversary during Chanukah in 2013.

When I wanted to be a nun in high school I prayed feverishly for guidance, happiness, connection with God and the wellbeing of my mom, dad and brothers and sisters. Now my prayers are not so much requests for anything so much as they are decrees that all is well and in divine order and flow.

I no longer pray for a divine connection. I now give thanks for the divine partnership I share. My responsibility in that partnership is to take the best care of myself and let Great Spirit do the rest. That's my part—to make sure I'm healthy, balanced, clear, loving and compassionate, with myself and with others.

When I'm challenged in any way, I remind myself of this commitment. I confirm that all is well and trust that everything is in divine flow, and that I am a part of this flow as long as I am willing to trust it unconditionally and do my part.

I don't add the condition of having to have my life circumstances turn out a certain way. I do pray that my gifts and talents be used in service for the highest and best for everyone I encounter. And I pray for peace, abundance, wholeness and love for all beings, everywhere.

Most of the time my prayer is giving thanks for the fullness of divine supply as I allow my heart and every cell of my being to be filled with gratitude. I breathe this gratefulness in and out of my heart, feeling love and the fullness of all good things. And then I send that love from my heart out into the world.

For many years I've cultivated what I call the Practice of the Presence of God, relying on the knowledge that the unseen Spirit of the Divine is all-present—in, with, and through the entire cosmos, always and everywhere—and that my physical body is a vessel for this Spirit.

Recently I developed a Rosary honoring Mary Magdalene and the sacred union—the partnership of Logos and Sophia incarnate in Jesus and Mary Magdalene. The Magdalene Rosary has seven groups of seven prayers honoring the Magdalene and seven Gospel Mysteries of Mary Magdalene encouraging us to meditate on her story, the archetypal heroine's journey and the individual soul's quest for union with God. In praying and meditating with this Rosary, we honor Jesus and Mary Magdalene, who embody the ancient mythology of the Sacrificed Bridegroom and his Beloved.

The prayers said with the Magdalene Rosary are similar to those of the traditional Marian Rosary.

1. The Prayer to the Source of Life (said on each introductory bead, and after citing of the mystery being contemplated) is the familiar Our Father prayer. Only the first line is changed to: O Mystery of Life, Birther of all that is...

2. The Magdalene Prayer (repeated on each of seven beads during contemplation of the appropriate mystery):

Dear Mary Magdalene, love incarnate,
Sacred Vessel, Holy Grail,
Chosen were you from all women,
And blessed is your union with Jesus.
Dearest Bride and Beloved of Christ,
Show us the Way of the heart.

3. Glory to the Source, the Force, and the Presence (said after each group of seven prayers before citing the next mystery).

Glory be to the Source, and to the Force,
And to the loving Presence.
As it was in the Beginning, is now and forever
shall be, world without end.

These prayers are repeated while meditating on the Magdalene Mysteries:

The Seven Gospel Mysteries of Mary Magdalene

1. Mary meets Jesus and is healed of seven demons.
2. Mary's tears move Jesus to raise her brother Lazarus from the tomb.
3. Mary anoints Jesus at the banquet at Bethany and wipes his feet with her hair.
4. Mary follows the Way of the Cross.
5. Mary stands with the Virgin Mother at the foot of the Cross.
6. Mary meets Jesus resurrected at the tomb on Easter morning.
7. Mary carries the Good News of the Resurrection to the Apostles.

Inspired by the world-affirming, action-oriented spirituality of Ignatius of Loyola, the founder of the Jesuits, I find that in my experience of prayer I naturally begin in a spirit of thanksgiving, savoring the intensity and abundance of Divine goodness that is poured into my life. It is in this stance of gratitude that I become mindful of the ways I feel blessed for the gifts of creation, life, sentience, sensitivity to goodness, truth and beauty, and by the utterly gratuitous ways that God's presence manifests in each moment.

I perceive this presence in the subtlest gestures of kindness, especially the kindness that happens spontaneously, or amongst strangers. I perceive it in the simplest pleasures: the time I spend walking outdoors between home and office; the quiet that comes over me when I turn off the radio and choose to be present to the silence of solitude; in moments of profound connection with others, especially those who are very different from myself.

And, taking stock of this abundance, I can't help but feel that I know, at some level, Christ's own experience as being beloved of God. I think of this dynamic of prayer as the way of fullness, the *Via Positiva* that reassures me that sensuality, imagination and the body are intended as blessings and as means of coming to acknowledge the Divine presence here and now. This act of paying attention to Divine abundance often leads me not only to express gratitude, but also to a deep and overwhelming desire to be generous in response— to offer myself back to God.

At the same time, acknowledging my desire to be more generous, more willing, freer and available to be used by God, I also recognize my attachments, my fears and the tendencies of my ego to serve its own interests. The sense of gratitude for such unmerited fullness nudges me toward the way of emptiness, the path of surrender and self-emptying in love that Paul describes in Christ as *kenosis*. This path of silence, of spareness, of stripping down is manifested in contemplative traditions such as the *Via Negativa*. When I am most open and spacious of heart, I perceive the Divine presence as well in moments of grief, disappointment and failure because, indeed, I am most aware of my contingency in these unbidden trials. This contingency is a path of connection to the One who creates and sustains me in love.

For me, prayer in its entirety involves both of these dimensions, not because they are human, but rather, because the paths of abundance and self-emptying are the dynamics of the Divine one who lives and moves and has being in us.

I try to let my voice speak for my heart—mostly in silence.

Every morning, as soon as I wake up, I pray before I leave the room I have slept in. I reach out and implore, using specific names of gods, goddesses, saints, teachers, family, friends and enemies, asking them to bless me and in turn giving them blessings. Prayer keeps me company throughout the day and during my dreams at night. I pray to become a better person and I need all the help I can get, so prayer is pretty much 24/7 for me.

I usually pray alone in silence or while walking among people on the street, but when the blessed opportunity arises, I will pray out loud or sing while in a group. All chances to pray are blessed opportunities.

Prayer is talking to God, conversing with God, singing to God, loving God, thanking God, asking to be made an instrument, asking to be made more humble and more available, asking for the skills to help contribute to the happiness and liberation of all beings, including animals. Prayer is a blessing received and given.

Prayer should always be done with the intention of getting to know yourself. When you finally become yourself, you will have everything. But on this journey towards becoming who we are, we at some point realize that we just don't know what is good for ourselves. We then start praying to bring into conscious awareness everything that is still unconscious.

I feel that prayer should be first and foremost a request, asking that every part of our personality that is still hidden and prevents us from embodying peace may come out into the open. Ask to see your responsibility whenever you find yourself at an impasse with someone. Ask to see your part in the conflict—commit yourself to wanting to see it, as much as doing so may wound your personal vanity. If you ask with wholeness, for the sake of truth itself, then God is revealed instantly. You then naturally pray for union, asking to become one with the Divine: *"May I be one with You. May the wave dissolve itself into the ocean."*

Silence is a vital element in creating a field of prayer. Be still and center your mind on the Divine. You may perform your prayers, but then again return to quietude. The answers you seek may emerge from this space of silence, or they can come at any other moment of your day. Be open to the signs around you: they are the language of existence speaking through synchronicity. This is the way that God speaks with you.

You will know that God has indeed answered your prayers, and that you have accessed the real self, when the answer you are seeking for actually arrives. But answers only come when you are able to overcome the ever-present resistance, the ever-present "no" to God. This "no" arises from images created in our minds and it indicates that we still have much difficulty in sustaining pleasure, since our vital energy has been "married" with negativity.

When we say "yes" with our whole being, we experience a flow of wisdom that answers all our questions. I feel that the clearest way to know that the Divine is manifesting is that we experience joy. Joy is a natural outcome of inner peace, which comes about when we are inhabited by the Divine.

Go on praying for all the darkness to be illuminated. The purpose of prayer is to increase your personal coefficient of light. It doesn't matter where you are, or what your situation may be. *Just call for God, and God will come. God is your best friend.*

In explaining the *sankalpa*, the promise of our lineage, Sri Sachcha Baba Maharajji, my beloved Guruji and spiritual master teacher, makes a prayer that always brings me a fresh new teaching:

"Oh Lord, remove from me this veil of evil tendencies. I am not powerful, but I am connected to You who are almighty. Your light enters me and I receive your wisdom. Any wrath, greed, envy and attachments disappear in the light of your wisdom. On the very day that your sight falls upon me, my lower nature and my human limitations shall be transformed into divine nature. My transformation is in your hands alone. Have compassion for me, come to me wherever I may be and reach through this veil.

"Wherever I go, I feel anxious, because I realize that I am just spinning around in the circles of ignorance. Oh Lord, protect me, save me, make me one with you! Help me to stop dreaming. Bring me to you. I hear it said that you are endowed with compassion, filled with goodness, and that forgiveness is your very nature. To give me this is your goal. So how can I possibly be without it? Oh Lord, my illusion is created by none other than you yourself. Tell me: can I possibly destroy it through my own efforts? Oh Lord! Test me no further. Break into pieces this chain of illusion that has plagued me for countless lifetimes. This veil that creates a world of differences can be burned to ash through your knowledge, all with a simple look from you."

Continue dialoguing with the Divine in this way, until there is no further need for such communication because there is no longer any distance between you and God, for you have fully embodied your own inherent divinity. You then pray merely by dancing along with the flowers fluttering in the breeze. Your prayer becomes simply being entirely present, here and now.

For many years I have spent many hours a day in silent communion with the Divine.

Not a day goes by that I do not, several times a day, take an hour or two—or often even three, sometimes eight, nine or ten hours, even whole days or several consecutive days—without worldly distractions and communications, to drop deep within, in my silent prayer communion, speaking with the Divine, asking how may I serve, listening, learning.

Everything I do is in prayer: I create sacred art in prayer, I write in prayer, I teach and heal in prayer, I mother in prayer, I walk on the beach in prayer, I cook and dance in prayer.

And God, the Divine, answers my prayers, revealing Its light, Its truth, weaving Its loving presence in the fabrics, in the prose and the poetry, the healing and the blessing.

I live in prayer.

My life is a prayer.

jeff brown

I pray by honoring my divine purpose, encoded in the soul-scriptures that live at the core of my being. Those scriptures are composed of a vast array of callings, archetypal transformations, key relationships and lessons that I am here to embody and learn through. The moment I honor any aspect of my divine purpose, the "soulular" phone turns on and there is a more direct interface between me and the Divine Mother. She calls to me, I call to her and my angels broker the deal. Our pipeline to divinity, the soulular phone connects our individual path to Universal Consciousness. The more inner work we do to clear the lines, the clearer the connection.

I pray best looking out my west window. A candle burns on the windowsill if it's dark, throwing shadows on the exquisite Mexican *latilla* ceiling of my log cabin. In the daytime I can see fifty miles away, across the San Luis Valley to the San Juan Mountains. Sometimes there are coyotes, elk or antelope. There are always deer, ravens and pinon jays. Day or night, I sit in silence, looking out the window, basking in the Presence.

My favorite description of God comes from William McNamara, the Carmelite priest who taught me so much about prayer in my forty years of monastic life. (I am no longer a monk.) Calling God *Personal Passionate Presence*, he said that the only response to Personal Passionate Presence is our own personal passionate presence. So I have learned to sit in silence, passionately present to the moment, in the fullness of my unique personhood, as who I simply am: Tessa. In the silence I feel the Presence surrounding me. I am immersed in it. I am one with it. It fills me and "speaks" to me, but not in words.

I name this Presence "God," having no trouble with God-language. Sometimes words come to mind, arising from my heart. They seldom move to my lips. Still in silence, I thank and praise God, and above all, love God. Sometimes there are tears, sometimes laughter—yes, out loud. I'm grateful for the day and night, the sun and snow, the animals and birds, the hard work and good play, the comedy and tragedy, the joys and sorrows that fill my life and the life of the whole world.

The world is always present in the silence of my hermitage and the stillness of my heart. For although there may be no one else sitting embodied with me in the solitude, the whole world is present to me in the Presence there.

I began praying with Hail Marys, Our Fathers, and Acts of Contrition, delivered on my knees with eyes closed and palms pressed together, seeking a God I was taught existed outside of myself. Later I turned to mantras and chants, postures and rituals in search of a more direct connection to the Oneness within. Reflections, envisionings, meditations, mind- and mood-altering drugs, Holotropic Breathwork and Tantric sex are also forms of prayer that I have and continue to practice in search of "the peace that passeth all understanding."

Today my path is one the good Dr. Jung recommended. I seek to replace believing with knowing. So now I pray by listening to the still, small voice within. I pray when I sculpt, write, make love, share what I know and celebrate nature with an open, curious heart. I pray when I remember that God/Oneness is in all of the things I have ever done, failed to do and have yet to do. I pray, when I remember, to be grateful, compassionate, generous and intimate with others. I pray when I feel pain—my own and others—and when I take risks, lose my way and have the courage to accept the limitations of being in the human experience. I pray when I surrender to not knowing and to silence and have the wit to experience awe in the face of the ordinary. I pray when I live my truth and when I admit its limitations. In short, I pray when I am faithful to that part of the great song that can only be sung through me in this often confounding and yet extraordinary miracle that I call my life.

I feel blessed.

Although it may appear strange, I don't really take time to pray. I feel a special contact with God left unspoken, and I feel the presence of God in my everyday life.

I don't really know whether or not God exists. I do know in my heart that Spirit exists, and there is a Spiritual reality which is way bigger than I am and much broader than what I can perceive with my physical senses. I feel the presence of Spirit during most of my conscious moments. I appreciate this awareness of Spirit like I appreciate the fresh air I love to breathe and the clean water I love to drink. Since I turned fifty years of age, my priority in life is to engage in activities which bring me closer to Spirit, which broaden my awareness of Spirit, and which enable me to communicate with Spirit. I am now sixty-six years old. I do not have anything to say about prayer, but I can say that Prayer is involved in all of these activities described below.

Prayer in the garden: I have planted a crop of blue corn each year for over twenty years. The corn seed was first gifted to me by Navaho women who came to teach the midwives of my community a Blessing Way ceremony. The Navahos told us that the blue corn was the most precious thing they had in their world and that every drop of water fed to their corn plants had been carried by hand. This corn keeps me praying all year. I pray when preparing the land for planting, I pray when planting each seed, I pray when weeding and feeding the plants, I pray when observing the plants pollinating, I pray when harvesting the corn, I pray when hanging the ears up in my barn to dry, I pray when taking the seeds off the cobs, and I pray when turning the handle of my grinder to grind the corn. I pray each time I gift the ground corn to the midwives and to other people who intend to make offerings. I pray and make offerings with corn often to feed the Spirits of the Earth. I have altars in my house and on my land with corn offerings.

Daily prayers: I greet each day with a vocal "good morning" to the Spirits of my home; my land; my family; my ancestors, if I happen to wake up at home; or the Spirits of whatever place I happen to be, if I am not at home. I give thanks for my life and ask the Spirits to help me all day to do my life in a good way. Throughout the day, I give gratitude to Spirit each time I eat food or drink water or a beverage. I am in constant prayer while driving (three times each week I commute one hundred and fifty miles round trip) for my safety and the safety of everyone else on the road. At day's end, I soak in hot water and meditate quietly so as to give myself the opportunity to hear whatever Spirit has to tell me.

Weekly prayers: I have a *chanunpah* (pipe), which was given to me by a Lakota Elder. Each week I take about an hour or two during which I fill the *chanunpah*, sit and pray with it and smoke it. This praying time includes the singing out loud of traditional Lakota prayer songs, the saying of words from my heart, and the listening silently to the inner reflection of my heart.

Emergency practice: Throughout the year I receive information from people I know (family, friends, community) or from people I do not even know, that someone needs prayers or healing. My practice is to fill the *chanunpah* and to place it on my altar for four days, during which I pray for the person needing prayers or healing. I smoke the pipe at the end of the four days. This is a Lakota practice given to me almost twenty years ago when I received my *chanunpah*. This happens at least a couple of times each month, and it gives me an opportunity to use my *chanunpah* in addition to the regular use I get with the weekly prayers.

Monthly prayers: I maintain a sweat lodge on my land. Each month, I lead a sweat lodge ceremony for the prayers of the people who attend (between eight and thirty people come to the ceremony). We sweat in the traditional Lakota way with songs, *chanunpah*, cedar, rocks, water and our prayers for the good life of the Earth and Her People. The ceremony ends with *Wopila*, a ceremonial meal eaten in gratitude to the Spirit.

Seasonal prayers: Four times a year, I take an all-day walk on one of the four local mountains within a one- or two-hour drive from my home. I spend the whole day climbing and walking on the mountain. At some point, I create an altar out of rocks and wood, and I make offerings of blue ground corn, tobacco, chocolate and a small amount of money. I pray all day while taking in the beauty of nature, and I make the offerings with the intention of pleasing the Spirits and asking for help with my economy, prosperity, good health and loving relationships with all creation.

Four times a year, on the Equinoxes and Solstices, I sit up with my all-night medicine circle to pray around a sacred fire for the good life of the People. This circle comprises close to a hundred people from all over the country, and between twenty and thirty-five people show up for each circle ceremony. Three of these circles happen in California, and for the Autumnal circle ceremony I travel to New Mexico. These circle ceremonies conclude with *Wopila*.

Additionally, on the night of the Winter Solstice, about a hundred people gather on my land for an evening ceremony to light candles and welcome the return of sunlight and longer days with our prayers for the New Year. And on the first Sunday in May, three hundred people gather on my land to dance around the maypole with our prayers honoring the Spirit of Fertility.

Once a year, I travel to the Lakota Reservation at Rosebud, South Dakota, for two weeks of ceremony comprising the *hanblecheya* (vision quest), purification and Sundance. These ceremonies are under the direction of an intercessor (medicine man) who places me out on a remote hill for the *hanblecheya* for one or two days (crying for a vision) with no food or water. Most of the other days are filled with sweat lodges, fasting, prayer and numerous tasks in preparation for the last four days of Sundance, during which I am praying while dancing for four days while pierced and roped to the Sacred Tree of Life.

Tobacco ties: The Lakota have taught me the practice of tying little bundles of tobacco wrapped in fabric and tied onto a string in various colors representing the compass directions and various Spirits. I spend time tying these tobacco ties each month while saying a prayer with each tie. Each year I grow a portion of the tobacco used in these ties, in each of the sweat lodge fires and in each of the medicine circle fires. The tobacco provides me with many opportunities to pray while growing it, while drying/curing it, and while using it in prayer ceremonies and making the prayer ties.

Life is a prayer. We often pray before meals, sometimes in the morning before we get out of bed, sometimes at night, or whenever we need to attune to Divine Presence. Rather than asking for what we want, we surrender always to "Let Your will be done." Here is a typical prayer:

"Heavenly Father and Universal Mother, we are so grateful for all your help and blessings. Help us to know your will and do your will. Help us to honor you in all and be a comfort to those in need. We are here to serve the Divine and ask that you use us well. Blessed be."

I use several forms of prayer because I love forms. We're incarnated and that's a great gift, so to be able to use form is a great help in "sacramentalizing" all aspects of our lives. My essential form of prayer is more a "resting in being prayed" rather than an active praying. In the mystical Christian contemplative tradition, they might call this "passive contemplation," but it doesn't really need any formal label to it. It has more to do with deeply resting in the source of all—whatever one might call that. For me, it's a ground of love, as the ground of existence. What emerges or arises from that is a spontaneous upwelling of silence, praise and gratitude and perhaps a sense of expansion—a numinous experience, for sure, difficult to capture in words.

From my background in Catholicism, as a nun, the whole idea of "me" doing the praying always took a backseat to attention to that "One" who is always already praying. Prayer might be called the breath of the universe. For me, it's aligning with that breath, surrendering in some way. If I have any "goal" in my prayer, it might be availability as a transformational vehicle—to serve in creation, in whatever way I am called to do. I know that prayer affects creation. How it does this—well, I can only speculate.

The forms of prayer that I've been instructed in from my spiritual teacher since 1985 comes out of the more Eastern Hindu tradition. I'm very partial to praying the Name of God. Let's face it, like anybody in this chaotic world, I run around from appointment to appointment, I drive around here and there, and my mind obsesses and focuses and gets drained of its attention so easily. So in this particular age and time, the repetition of an internal prayer is extremely useful to keeping the highest intention possible. I repeat the Name of God, much like in the Prayer of the Heart or the Jesus Prayer. These forms keep the pilgrim focused on his or her intention, focused on the source of all. It is my experience that the sounds of the various Names of God do have an impact on the neurological system of the body and do align us to an energy that opens what needs to be opened and aligns what needs to be aligned.

Prayer at specific times and in specific places is a part of my daily practice. But prayer also spontaneously arises when, for instance, one hears in the news that there are fires raging in New Mexico or wars in Afghanistan. What can I do from my desk in the office or my post at the kitchen sink except to hold my intention for those afflicted, and breathe and repeat an internal prayer in the Name of God to bless those who need courage in this particular time and energy to work that. I generally don't find myself praying for things like, "Oh God, please make the fire stop." I've never been oriented toward praying to ask for some kind of divine intervention. That's always seemed really presumptuous. However, just holding in compassion and blessing the whole situation—the situation of the Earth, the situation of the individuals involved—is important because we all need courage and strength and joy in any kind of challenging situation.

Prayer really becomes a way of life. It's possible in each relationship, with each person who walks in your door and with each bit of news you hear. You "witness and bless," as Rabbi Zalman Schachter-Shalomi would say. You witness and bless in everything you do. Prayer can become how you breathe. How you communicate. How you align yourself with the ground of being, the ground of love.

For me, prayer is also silent sitting for fifty minutes to an hour every morning and occasionally stopping during the day for quiet periods, contemplative reading of the great teachings, the use of prayer beads. I always loved the Rosary when I was more ardently a Roman Catholic; I love to have something in my hands because I love form. I use mantras, I use prayer beads, I love to do yoga, because for me, that's the body in prayer—it's exciting to know that prayer is not only the mind, that it's the work of every cell in the body.

Singing, chanting the psalms—the psalms are really wonderful—are other great forms of prayer. Song and chant create a vibration within myself, certainly, but I also experience that this vibration touches something in creation. I don't know how; we don't know the technology of this, but I just know that the ethers are full of static and getting more and more all the time, and that filling the ethers with chant—with the Name of God, with blessing—well, it wouldn't hurt!

I love going on retreat. Prayer retreat is an essential part of my year. What a privilege to take a couple of weeks to go away and do nothing except to practice in the sense of devoting the whole day to prayer and study of the great teachings and to immerse myself in what lies at the center once again.

I would like my life to make a difference—I think we all would. Some of us will do this through our active lives, as we are like the finger cells in this great mystical body. And some of us are quieter, more contemplative cells, and our prayer will be our contribution to creation. I really trust the great contemplative traditions, Eastern and Western, which have sustained the Earth for as long as they have, and certainly have served as sanctuary to vast numbers of people throughout the world. Just knowing that there are people in prayer throughout the world sustains us and provides a counterpoint to the insanity that we live in.

For me, it's not about doing "the big praying thing." It's about relaxing into that which already is. And it takes a while to learn. But we are up to it.

The meaning of prayer and how we practice it has been a driving issue for me for as long back as I can remember. I define it as "a radical response to life."

If prayer is a radical (meaning "root" or "deep") response to life, then I am praying when I write a book, do research, lecture, walk silently by water, be still, dance, chant phrases, utter prayers, go into contemplation, observe children or puppies at play, make love, undergo awe and amazement or grief and suffering or angry powers that be by protesting.

Prayer is what we do out of our depths, out of our roots. Or whatever we do to return to those depths, where, as Meister Eckhart puts it, "God is at home; it is we who have gone out for a walk."

Prayer is silence, and prayer is breaking the silence. Prayer is moral outrage, and prayer is steering our anger in a creative and responsible fashion to divert those forces that have brought the moral outrage alive in us; prayer is our creativity, our birthing alternatives, our bringing delight to others.

Prayer is the amazement and reverence and gratitude that are awakened in me at the very awareness that I am gifted with existence within this awe-filled cosmos with its 13.8-billion-year history. No wonder Meister Eckhart can say, "If the only prayer you say in your whole life is 'Thank You,' that would suffice."

So I try to "pray always," as Paul recommended—not by saying prayers all the time but by trying to live life (many mystics say God is life) out of my depths, out of the *Via Positiva* (awe, joy and gratitude), the *Via Negativa* (silence, grief and letting go), the *Via Creativa* (what we give birth to) and the *Via Transformativa* (our work for justice and compassion). We never get there. But hopefully, the journey is also the way.

One might say that saying prayers is second person, meditation is no person, worship is third person and overall, prayer as a radical response to life is first person, as in: "I vow to commit myself to a radical response to life."

I pray with my body. Prayer becomes deeper through action, because what I'm doing with my body is my prayer. Prayer is what I'm doing with my child, what I'm putting in my body, what I'm emitting through words, how I'm choosing to use my energy. Prayer is embodied and expresses itself through relationship and action.

Individually, sometimes it's time for retreat, sometimes it's time to be a new mom and sometimes it's time to be an old lady, knitting mantras into a blanket. Each season calls us to do different things. We want to enter into our bodies and integrate our intentions and our awareness and our gestures through our bodies and express from there. It's really important to integrate ourselves and to connect with the "other."

Together, we are all bringing our bodies, our consciousness, our intentions and our intelligences together. We are praying together, with our bodies, our actions and a network that we are creating on every level we can.

In relationship, we have to make these direct links and weave this net as beautifully as we can, with as much integrity as we can, because everybody is needed. And every prayer we bring forth is going to be a healing force in the world. In relationship to all the destruction that's happening, we need each other. We need everybody. We know that's our prayer.

This is something we need to do, and it requires everybody, whether we succeed or not. Everyone's actions toward that would be prayer. That is beautiful.

bruce sanguin

My life is prayer, a moment-by-moment summoning up of my most loving and creative response to divine initiative. Prayer is how my body, heart and mind resonate with the shifting circumstances and challenges that the universe throws my way. In sadness, I weep. When I look deeply into the eyes of another, my heart fills with love and my eyes overflow with another kind of tears. In fear, I contract, witness my withdrawal and ask for support. In confusion, I seek intellectual clarity. My understanding is that the creative, loving divine presence is within both the circumstance and my response. The end goal of prayer as one's life's work is the capacity to assume increasing degrees of responsibility as a life artist. At any given moment, the shape of our life, our relationships, our attitude, and behaviors are a perfect snapshot of our artistry. It can be sobering to take a fearless inventory of our life and realize that we are painter of the portrait.

All spiritual traditions speak of freedom as a fruit of the life of prayer. The paradox is that freedom increases in direct proportion to our capacity to take responsibility. Absolute freedom is ultimate responsibility and vice versa. When we realize that nobody and no circumstance has the power to steal our freedom, we break the bonds of victimhood and shift from being creatures to creators—"creaturehood" is transcended, yet included. Understanding one's life as a continual prayer is the royal road to this wisdom.

One of the labels I allow myself is "evolutionary mystic." What this means is that I know myself to be one with the cosmic processes that gave birth to me. I am the cosmic evolutionary impulse to transcend itself and realize deeper expressions of truth, beauty and goodness. It is, I am, we are—a process that has come to conscious awareness after 13.7 billion years. We are the presence of this universal creativity seeking to transcend itself and realize greater depths of beauty, goodness and truth. The "self" is not a discrete thing waiting to be found. It is not hiding. Like it or not, it is on public display. Rather, the journey is about expressing oneself as a manifestation of divine, universal creativity.

To use theological language, we are the divine heart and mind enjoying the ecstasies and devastations of what it means to be human. This practice of life as prayer helps us to shift out of the illusion of separation and the suffering caused by this isolated self-sense. We expand into an understanding and experience of self as a single, unified and unifying process seeking to give birth to a unique human (you) and, on a collective level, to the emergence of the new human. As the presence of the universe in human form evolving, we are its intimate expression. We are a living, learning universe, constantly experiencing and adapting to shifting life conditions. Rather than organizing our lives to cushion the crises, prayer as life's work reframes the various crises of life, planetary, relational and personal. These are reimagined and undergone as provocations that elicit new and necessary intelligences that will increase our capacity to make of our lives a more radiant offering, serving the ongoing evolution of the planet.

In my tradition, there is one prayer that encapsulates all that I am saying in a nine-word sentence, uttered by Mary, mother of Jesus: "Let it be to me according to your word" (Luke 1:38). This could be shortened to a single word, offered with sincerity at the beginning of our day. "Yes" to the birth of the sacred, in, through, and as me; "yes" to the birth of deeper intimacies in my relationships and community; "yes" to a collective shift in consciousness so that our social, political, economic, and technological systems are realigned in service to this one Earth community; "yes" to the divine invitation to assume, with grace and humility, responsibility for this sacred emergence. "Yes," and let it begin with me.

What would love say?

Love would say open yourself AS the prayer.

Love would say breathe...

Breathe and lean intimately towards the temple of your own heart.

Breathe directly into your own heart, imagining that with each breath your heart opens petal by petal by petal, like a beautiful rose unfurling in the soft morning light.

Feel the rainbow dewdrops on the petals of your own tender, loving heart.

As your heart opens with each breath, start to see the golden light begin to shine in the very center of your heart—feel and see your heart filling with delicious, warm, golden light.

Focus your breath here, and as you do, feel your heart begin to spill over with golden light.

Feel this golden light as it begins to stream though your body.

It is a golden ray of light that is dancing prayers deep into your blood, bones, muscles and cells. It is a golden ray of light that vibrates the prayer of love through you and beyond you. It is the golden ray of light that dances your prayer into the universe.

From this space slowly open the eyes of your heart to gaze upon your world with the eyes of love.

Now, every time you breathe, bring your awareness to your own being as a living prayer. See with the eyes of love,

Touch with the hands of love,

Speak with the lips of love.

Let your being become the living payer of love.

The way I pray is quite straightforward, but it needs a little background to provide it with some context and spiritual meaning. But first, the prayer: In the morning when I get up, I sit on the side of my bed, close my eyes and ask Spirit to allow me to serve it that day. I ask, "Spirit, guide me throughout the day in how to better serve Thy will on Earth." At night before I go to bed I thank Spirit for having given me the opportunity to be of service that day, and I ask for further guidance the following day.

This type of prayer comes out of the emerging tradition of evolutionary spirituality. This spiritual lineage stretches back to the teachings of Sri Aurobindo and Teilhard de Chardin, and is being evolved today by teachers like Andrew Cohen, Craig Hamilton and Michael Dowd, among many others. Evolutionary spirituality views the cosmos as Spirit-in-action; God is not only the ground of Being, but is also fully immanent within the creative life process itself. The cosmos is seen as a single, unfolding event of which we're an intimate part, and we're called to be co-creators with this dynamic process. The goal of the spiritual path is to connect to the part of us that's always already alive with this evolutionary impulse, this Yes to life and growth and change that is our deepest self. We're called to serve Spirit's will, to be vehicles for Spirit's next move, and we come to feel most fully alive and most complete when we learn to align ourselves in this way.

The prayer I do is a sincere reminder to always keep this as my primary life context. I wake up with the intention to serve Spirit throughout my day whenever or however I'm called to do so. This takes a certain receptivity to life, an openness to what's unfolding around me. I might unexpectedly be asked to take part in a new project, and I open to this possibility; I might make eye contact with someone in a way that tells me intuitively that I should speak to them, so I do. If I'm open and sensitive to what's happening around me in this way, my experience is that life becomes very dynamic and unpredictable in the best way. Life becomes an unfolding adventure, and I find a certain serenity knowing that I'm not ultimately in charge.

One thing I've learnt through doing this kind of prayer and living in this manner, is that if you offer your services up to Spirit, you will be utilized. Doors will start to open, connections will begin to be made and Spirit will make use of you to the precise extent you are willing and ready. It's a blessed way to live, for which I am grateful.

I love when prayer just happens...for me, this is when I am overwhelmed with gratitude.

Often, when I am alone in nature, it just comes over me and feels like a childlike joy—it almost takes my breath away. There are no words in my prayer; there is, however, a fullness of heart which spills over into a big smile—inner as well as outer. Also, it often happens when I go to bed at night and I lie on my back, just being there with the question, "Are you ready to die?" Which means...am I complete with everything? And again it comes back—the feeling of gratitude that everything is taken care of. Just to lie in bed in gratitude, with no particular words, this is my prayer. And last, but definitely not least, is the feeling of overwhelming bliss and joy while singing and chanting together with my beloved Miten and the people who come to sing with us. To be lost in the sound our voices create together and to enjoy the sound vibrations of the mantras and Miten's sacred songs; to express the gratitude through the music that arises out of the moment, out of that particular combination of souls—this is my bliss. This is my prayer.

miten

Prayer is not something one "does"—it is not an asking or a "doing"... it is a wonderment, a state of innocence, a state of grace, a sense of deep gratitude.

Not knowing to whom the gratitude is addressed.

Not knowing whose hand is hidden behind every grass leaf. In such a mysterious and wondrous realm, all is given and all is received.

This is prayer.

Prayer for Words

"My voice restore for me."
—Navajo

Here is the wind bending the reeds westward,
The patchwork of morning on gray moraine.

Had I words I could tell of origin,
Of God's hands bloody with birth at first light.
Of my thin squeals in the heat of his breath,
Of the taste of being, the bitterness,
And scents of camasroot and chokecherries.

And, God, if my mute heart expresses me,
I am the rolling thunder and the bursts
Of torrents upon rock, the whispering
Of old leaves, the silence of deep canyons.
I am the rattle of mortality.

I could tell of the splintered sun. I could
Articulate the night sky, had I words.

In the ceremonial dance, we pray with our bodies, running to the tree at the center of the sacred hoop and dancing back to our place in the circle, always facing the tree, honoring life. We hold feathers up to the sky and blow bone whistles as we dance to say, "Great Mystery, I am here. I send a voice. I send a prayer with my feet on this sacred Earth."

Over and over we run to the tree, following the heartbeat of the drum from the first light of dawn until that blazing ball of light falls beneath the horizon. We do not stop. We do not eat or drink. We run forward and dance backward, our eyes always on the tree, always turned toward life.

At the start, my intent is clear, my prayers having been prepared during days of fasting and meditation. I focus my attention on the longings of my heart: for healing, for the wellbeing of those I love, for wisdom in my work, for peace on the planet, for courage in community. I dance in gratitude for life, for all that we are given, for the beauty of this planet. My heart and my feet are light. I feel as if I could dance forever, over and over to the tree and back.

The sky turns from pale blue to the brilliant hue that almost hurts your eyes to look at as the sun climbs in the sky. My back begins to ache and my intentions blur. The prayers I have held in my mind become jumbled. Sweat pours down my face. My legs cramp.

I think of those who have pain in their bodies every day—those who are ill or injured, hungry, without medical care, alone or frightened, in areas of armed conflict. And I dance for them—that they may find peace, that they may be well.

I dance for my sons, and then I dance for all parents and their children, remembering especially those who have lost children or live in fear of losing children to sickness or starvation, to domestic or military violence. I dance in gratitude for the beauty and miracle of birth and remember the other children of Grandmother Earth— her plants and animals, the water and air, the rocks and minerals.

And I dance for them, in gratitude for the beauty and sustenance they offer, asking that they be protected.

I give my body to the dance. My body is my prayer. Sometimes there is pain. Sometimes unexpected ease returns, and I dance with fresh energy, renewed from some unseen source. Resistance arises—the temptation to quit. The sun seems to stand still in the sky. I go to the tree one more time...and another...and another. Tears come and go. Exhaustion threatens to topple me. But I am there now without thought, all aspirations of being eloquent in my prayer, graceful in my dance sweated out, left behind. I stumble. I fall, coming down on one knee and struggle to get up.

This is how I pray, whether I am in a ceremonial dance or in the dance of an ordinary day. I get up and move toward life, often with a focused prayer in my heart, on my lips. I buy carrots and squash at the market, make a soup for lunch, talk with a friend who is grieving the loss of her husband, write a poem, answer emails, get my teeth cleaned, revise a chapter, pay the electricity bill...each move is another run to the tree, a prayer in motion.

Sometimes I am awake and aware, and I consecrate this run—this task—to what is larger and sacred, bringing mindfulness to my movements. I pay the electricity bill with a prayer of thanks for the means to do so and for the power that heats my home, cooks my food and brings light to the darkness. I add a prayer that we develop and use sustainable ways to provide that power—ways that do no harm to this planet, our home.

Sometimes awareness is buried in busyness or weariness and I forget to dedicate my actions or moments to the Sacred Mystery that sustains me. But still, I move toward life allowing my actions to become my prayer, hoping it is enough.

And sometimes in that ordinary day, as in the ceremonial dance, I come to my knees and struggle to rise. And where I am unable to get up, my prayer is in the curve of my back and the tears in my throat, in accepting the limits of what my small will can do. I ask for help, I surrender, and something lifts me, holds and carries me. Sometimes this happens all at once, taking my breath away with instantaneous transformation. And sometimes it is a slow and gentle lifting, almost imperceptible, until I find myself back on my feet once more, filled with gratitude and renewed faith.

This is how I pray. One day at a time. Dancing until I cannot and that which brought me here lifts me up and carries me forward. The prayer is in the life lived with awareness, in the intention and even in the forgetting so the remembering may come again. It is in the joy and the sorrow, the struggle and the surrendering, in the opening that comes as we move more deeply into life, over and over again.

wallace j. nichols

A Prayer to the Ocean

We stand at the edge of the sea. We say nothing. We breathe its salt, its oxygen. We see its blue or green or gray. We listen to the songs in its waves and its tide pools. We may dance. We feel its coolness. We step into the liquid, with all of our brothers and sisters of all time, with all of the elements of all time: the squid and the whales, the sea turtles and the dinoflagellates; the silver and copper, the manganese and sodium. We swim out as far as we can, knowing we'll have to return to the land.

I pray by first emptying my being and blessing and releasing my mind so I can be fully present in the moment. I call back all parts of my spirit—from past, present and future to be here NOW. Focusing my attention on my heart, I allow the unconditional loving presence that lives there to fill my body and my being until it expands and overflows into the space around me.

And then I begin to sing—and be sung. As I open my being and invoke ancient chants and mantras, spirit begins to move through me and fills the chalice of my being. As my own frequency rises, my ego begins to fall away and my essence takes dominion.

In this state of grace, I know we are one. From here, fear melts into the shadows. I call out to Spirit within and to the intelligence of the universe, asking that the highest good be served. I often pose a question that I sense requires deeper reflection and guidance. And then I listen with all of my being. I watch to see what inner impulses or sensations arise from the well of empty fullness at my center. Perhaps I am gifted with an image or a word, and I sit watching it blossom into clear seeing. Perhaps I receive a direct missive from the Goddess with her marching orders for my life or my community. And sometimes I just sit, allowing the silence and the inner music to fill me, nurture me and hold me tenderly. I steep like an ancient tea, drinking in this sacred nectar. Then I release it all back to the Cosmos. And I know that it is done. It is done. It is done. In the name of the One.

Blessed be.

Prayer covers such a wide range of communication with the invisible that I want to find new words that more precisely point to how I pray.

> Prayer in moments of gratitude is different from
> Prayer in moments of hope is different from
> Prayer in moments of delight is different from
> Prayer in moments of desperation and crisis.

I look at my history and observe: What I consider as prayer has changed and matured over the years. Even a decade ago I regarded and practiced prayer differently than today. Twenty years ago I sang; I chanted; I abandoned myself in calling, adoring, imploring, beseeching, repeating the ten thousand names of the Beloved in song. The Beloved is a name for God, love, harmony, beauty...the wonder of life.

Today, I recognize that prayer arises when I am fully present. Prayer is the stillness, the peace and oneness with what is. Prayer is a smile, a touch, the intimacy of being at one with the other—at one with the whole (atonement). Prayer includes and is beyond the emotional or rational realm.

How do I pray? The more I am faced with this question, the more I am finding myself *in* the mystery of a Koan (a question to be with, rather than to answer!) and very like the question: "Who am I?" My prayer is an essential quality, indistinguishable from who I am... present in expression, in stillness, in action and non-action.

I am resonant with the Zen, yoga and martial art-perspective of "practice" when I intentionally spend time being close to the Beloved—being aware, breathing, non-doing, leaning into emptiness, exploring asanas, running, hiking, moving. There seems to be a lot of doing, depending on the inner posture. My prayer is all about aliveness in presence and alignment with who I am. When I am inspired, when I sing, when I compose, when poetry comes through me, when I lead singing circles, when I am sitting in silence...I am in prayer!

Prayer does not end when the practice ends! I cannot distinguish where I end and prayer begins. Prayer is with me, I am prayer...prayer is the fragrance of my being. Prayer is who I am. Deep gratitude, joy and simplicity arise out of this and have become my life.

Our prayers are given upwards, much like the rising of smoke. Historically, many cultures have believed that smoke carries prayers upwards to the realm where the ancestors, angels and the divine reside. This includes smoke in all forms: incense smoke, smoke from herbs or smoke from a pipe.

The burning of fragrant herbs, barks, resins, woods and flowers was part of the religious and spiritual practice of many ancient cultures and still is. The word perfume is derived from the Latin *per fumum*, meaning "through smoke." "Let my prayer be set before thee as incense; and the lifting up of my hands as the evening sacrifice" (Psalm 141:3).

As a child I went to an all-girls monastery/boarding school. The Abbot granted me special permission to fill the role of altar boy. So I was an altar girl, and it was an important job to me, which I took very seriously. I was fascinated with incense. My favorite task was to prepare the incense censer (burner) with pieces of frankincense, and to see the clouds of sweet, fragrant smoke go upwards in the cathedral towards heaven. It was mysterious and special to me.

Since that time, the use of incense with my prayers has been a daily routine. I use incense for purifying the mind and the energy field as well as for creating a sacred space in which to commune with the divine.

I have always had a great love for, and personal relationship to, both incense and prayer. I feel that prayer should carry the feeling tone of one talking with God as a friend. The Sufi poet Rumi often spoke about God as a companion and friend and his love and devotion have always touched me deeply.

Incense is a helpful tool for me in accessing this devotional state of prayer. It is as if the incense passes through any veils and delivers my prayer and devotion to God. It is also noteworthy that certain scents have an immediate effect on brain chemistry and brainwave states, and one actually does enter another state of being.

I have traveled all over the world studying incense and plants, and I have visited many temples and sacred sites in Asia, India and the Orient. I have often watched in awe as people of every race and age lit candles and burned incense in total devotion and prayer to the divine.

I pray with fire. Over many decades, I have collected beautiful, colorful candleholders from around the world made of shell, stone, pottery, metal or glass. They suit many needs, moods, seasons and circumstances. Lighting candles is prayer as well as a way of tending seeds of light and hope in the darkness.

I pray with water, sometimes sprinkling it on the Earth as a blessing. When trees are badly injured in high winds, I anoint their bark from a little bottle of Grail water from Glastonbury.

I pray with dance, spinning like the cosmos, grounding myself in ancient patterns.

I pray with Buddhist and Hindu chants, or with sounds I make up.

I pray by extending my thanks to the universe, no matter how depressed I might be. I collect moments of gladness to be remembered with gratitude in dark times. Meister Eckhardt wrote, "If the only prayer one ever says is 'thank you,' it will suffice." A related Jewish prayer is: "Thank you for bringing me to this place." Especially when I feel tired, I look around my beautiful old house, its windows covered with ivy, and whisper those words.

When I cannot sleep, I pray in my mind, repeating the *Ave Maria* in Latin, over and over (but I omit *peccatoribus* because I see us as learners, not "sinners").

I pray using the Jewish concept of *Berakah*, a blessing one offers to everything—the dawn, the floor I walk upon, my cats, my trees and plants, my food, my books and work, the air I breathe, sunset, twilight, late night, stars, moon, weather spirits, seas, rivers, lakes, a glass of red wine.

These are all the ways I pray.

My way of praying changes over time. For the last few months, I have been looking at, smelling and hearing the sea. I find myself speaking to it: "Dear Teacher, thanks for showing me how to flow and splash as you do."

Blessings for the waters of the world.

I have been caring for a water altar in my home since 2001. We all know the importance of water, and that life is absolutely dependent upon it. I believe that healing the waters is essential. By bringing purity and harmony into the waters of the world, we can make fundamental changes, perhaps even in the way the collective thinks and lives.

To start your water altar, you can use any water that is available; however, I recommend that you make the gathering of that water as sacred and ceremonial as possible. You can create ritual at a nearby waterway, pond or lake, or even consciously draw tap water with the intention of sanctifying it through your prayers. I recommend that you choose a special bowl, the vessel that will grace the altar and hold the water.

I sing to the altar whenever I am praying there, and when I offer the water back into the pond, the river or wherever I go to change and renew it. The lyrics that have come to me are: *"I honor the sacred Altar. I honor the sacred Water. May it flow throughout the land. May it flow throughout the hearts of Man."* When you sit with your water altar and offer your prayers, you might receive a song of your own.

Whenever I stand at my water altar, I pray for the waters of the world. I pray that the waters flow clean and pure and that all people and all plants and creatures have enough clean, pure water to drink. I pray for those places that are in drought and those places that are in floods. I pray for the places where the waters have been fouled, and wherever there is pollution or danger of pollution. I send love and positive energy to the waters of the world, and I offer my breath and prayers with an open heart, in humility and gratitude for the waters of life, without which there would be no life. When I finish praying, I use a long crystal wand to stir the prayers into the water on my altar, which symbolizes all the Earth's waters. I ask that the prayers be multiplied ten thousand times.

There are times when I am distraught or upset, and I go to the water altar for solace and pray to the spirits of water for help. Water is a very strong conductor for the energies that we generate with and transmit from our hands. When I am working with the water altar, I almost always have my hands placed around the altar vessel, and I always open my heart and let the universal life force energy run through my hands. If you spend time listening, you will receive wisdom and guidance while in the presence of your water altar.

If there is one thing that life has taught me, it's to trust that even when it's hopeless, intense and scary, I still have earth beneath me, the air I breathe all around me, and I still have my thoughts—which I direct towards my devotion to service.

I make a daily practice out of observing the self—the *who* and *where* in me that is running the show. I pray to the Divine Mother, that she heal me and that she also pray to our Father on my behalf.

To do this, I must fully comprehend the ego. Then, I take responsibility for it and ask to be cleansed. I ask to be brought back to the heart, so I can give thanks, and move forward with courage and guidance.

I sublimate my energy into the heart and the mind, creating a pure path from my roots to my crown in hope that more light might enter and embody who I am.

There is also a daily prayer that I do. It takes less then five minutes, depending on how much I elaborate on it. Whether in the car, makeup chair or waiting room at the dentist, I refine myself from the inside out.

1. I start by anchoring down to the earth and sending a red light twenty feet into the Mother. I feel my connection to the pure earth. I affirm it: "I am supported and grounded by the earth in which I am founded."
2. I then begin to feel the element of water and I connect to my feminine, creative qualities, saying, "I surrender in devotion to the motion of the ocean and I celebrate as I create."
3. I then connect to my core, and visualize the center of the universe, harmonizing with the light inside me, saying, "I connect in harmony and balance at my core, so I can be more of what I came here to be."
4. I then start to feel my gratitude enhance my ability to open my chest with more breath, saying and feeling, "I breathe, believe and receive from my heart; in gratitude is where I start."

5. I allow my requests to be in service to the divine will. I focus on my throat and say, "I communicate so I can liberate, and I am free to be me."

6. I then feel the core of my brain being saturated with emptiness and openness, and I say a meditation: "I let go of all I know, so I can realize with my REAL EYES."

7. I then begin my prayer. I envision a crown at my head, and I say, "I open and align with the guidance of the Divine—I am one with the most high."

In this state, I trust any information that comes down and through me, and I vow to trust and enact any insight that I have. I vow to follow the promises I make to the Divine Mother and Father, and to listen to the pure, unending guidance that I am led by. I ask that I may be shown to live in service, to continue to grow in the consciousness and awareness of my being, and to strengthen my connection to my divinity. All for God, in all ways.

First, it's important to know what you are praying to. That has changed for me over the years. As a kid, I prayed to God via Hebrew prayers (with archaic English translations) in our local synagogue. Not much happened.

Later, as a Buddhist, I learned to pray to Buddhist patriarchs, matriarchs and bodhisattvas. The monks told us we were really praying to our own inner resources, and some vaguely articulated external spiritual forces. But it seemed like idol worship. Bowing to statues, photographs and paintings of all the aforementioned didn't help matters. Shamanism also felt like idolatry. Why pray for help from spirits? Why not pray to what they pray to?

For the last fifteen years, I've been studying Hebrew scripture and the associated commentaries. I couldn't escape the notion of God, but had little idea of what it meant, nor how to pray to God. Led by the hand by the medieval Jewish philosophers, the desire to know became the experience of seeking. This is a type of prayer—beseeching. "What are you, God?" "Where are You?" "How can I know You?"

Studying, thinking and just sitting gradually added onto beseeching the forms of thanksgiving, awe and praise. I say three little prayers off throughout the day: grace after meals, a prayer for the bereaved and a request for healing and salvation. The content is less important to me than is the acknowledgment of God's presence that they contain. "Don't ask for food when hungry; ask for God's mercy."

For many years I've called forth a beautiful Temple by the Sea through my morning meditation. I enter into the holy of holies, the inner sanctum, where I spend time with God in prayer. Afterwards, I engage in a profound process called Active Imagination, during which I receive guidance from this trusted source. I have filled shelves of beautiful journals with dialogue between God and myself. I ask the questions and God always provides wisdom, insight and clarity.

Lately, God shows up as Great Father or as Great Mother, Shekinah. It's like writing a play. I use M for Marcia, G for God and GM or S for Great Mother or Shekinah.

Here's what I wrote/received this morning:

Marcia: God?
God: Yes, my child?
M: What am I learning about believing?
G: That at one level it's useful and at another, not necessary. I am here, whether you believe it or not, but your believing allows you personally to trust.
M: I feel that when I use my will, I feel less of you.
G: You do, but this is part of your separation belief. I work through you.
M: So when I use my will to make something happen, why do I feel like it's me and not you?
G: There is no you and no me.
M: How may I know this?
G: Try it on. Say, "This is God working through me." And feel what happens.
M: To everything?
G: Try it on. Feel/experience yourself as me for moments each day.

Then I take the guidance, practice it and integrate it into my daily life. I used to pray that I would become enlightened before I die. Now I practice daily enlightenment in three easy steps.

1. Spend more time in the light—connected to God, laughing, in the sun, etc.

2. Spend less time in the dark—with fear, doubt, negative people or thoughts.

3. Practice living a virtuous life—with integrity at the Soul level.

The only prayers I know are "Thank you" and "Thy will be done." The odd thing is that I do not assume—or know—that there is anyone or any One to whom I am directing those prayers. A God? The universe? My own heart? Maybe it doesn't matter. Maybe that is the essence of faith. Like Socrates, I know nothing for certain. I don't know what happens to us when the body dies. I don't know where we came from or what destiny awaits us. But I choose to believe that all that happens is for our highest good and learning. Meantime, I say, "Thank you" and "Thy will be done."

I warn people who might hear me practicing that it is like "praying out loud." Some of the song will sound wonderful, but there are times when I need to go over and over one phrase, singing it again and again.

Each time I sing a phrase, I am exploring what that particular sequence of notes might do. How does the room feel when I sing it? What is the quality of silence in the moment right after I finish singing? How comfortable (or uncomfortable) is my body when I sing the phrase?

The answers to these questions remind me that my singing is merely a medium through which Spirit moves. Music is like the magician's wand, distracting those who listen from noticing the subtle works of Spirit embedded into those beautiful notes. We cannot resist that which we do not notice.

As I rehearse each song, I open to the spiritual wisdom within the music. I seek to be a channel for the song, and I take a moment to invite those angels who sat on the shoulder of the composer of the song to now sit with me as I sing. The sensation I have when this happens is that my singing becomes my prayer.

Sometimes the notes are quite strong and loud. When this happens, my entire body physically vibrates with the higher notes I learned to sing as an opera singer. Sometimes the notes are so soft that the air barely passes through my lips. The potency of these notes is palpable in the entire room. There is only a deep, rich silence meeting my ears. Spirit is present. And here I am also. What amazing company!

In prayer I return to that place inside that feels ever-connected and always home. It is a sanctuary of trusting that all things will work out for the best in the end, whatever the appearance may be, and I bring this awareness into my everyday life and present moments. This practice, which is ongoing, is not linked to a particular time or outer place.

Music—in particular, song and chant—is a way of helping to feel a connection to that sanctuary inside. The beauty of this practice is that it is wonderful to do on my own, but also to share with others. The resonant vibration of chanting together in harmony is an incomparable way to feel a deeper connection with humanity, with life and with the Great Song surrounding us.

Prayers reside in the heart, and song is a link there. One way of praying with others is to listen to someone's intention or request and respond with a new song with lyrics created as a fulfillment of their request, a confirmation of their intention and an honoring of their being. Anyone can do this—it is a natural act of empathic communication, not only the province of composers and songwriters. In this way, a musical blessing can be shared with others, which enriches our own prayer life as well.

My wish for you, the reader, is that your prayer life ever renews and returns you to your connection with the Great Song, however you relate to this universal birther, sustainer and dissolver of everything.

chris deckker

Prayer is how I communicate with the divine. It is how I can use the power of affirmation and intention in a focused way to recognize sacred space, invoke that sacred space, and then use the power of words and intention. The idea is to take this affirmation into all daily aspects of my life, so that all activity throughout my life and my moments throughout the day have prayerful reflection. I think, in essence, that prayer itself—or the technology of prayer, if you like—is a tool. The power of prayer can be used to harness the energy of the sacred and divine and create change and inspiration in your life. Within prayer, there is an aura of gratitude, wonder and thanks for the divine and for everybody in your life, and for all of the different realms that interact and intersect to create who you are on the planet.

Prayer doesn't necessarily have to have words or affirmations or intentions attached to it. It is the act of surrendering. When you are dancing and you're in the ecstatic space of surrender, you can harness the prayerful energy—the life force, if you like—and combine it on a collective level. Through Earth Dance, in the moment of that kinetic movement of dance and energy, the joyful expression of coming together, dancing and celebrating, we can create a moment of stillness, which we call the prayer for peace, affirming our intention for peace on the planet.

If you look at ancient times, community rituals and celebrations quite commonly had both dance and music components. People got together, danced and celebrated the ecstatic light. Whether the gathering was in honor of a seasonal change or the harvest, prayer had a musical component that was intrinsically linked to the ecstatic ritual or rite of passage being held in the ceremonial space.

If you look at our Christian culture today, music plays an important part in the church atmosphere through celebratory, ecstatic hymns and songs of praise. That's what inspired me when I was a child: hearing the voices and harmonies connecting in the church atmosphere. It gave me a deep sense of euphoria and a deep sense of, "Wow, this is my community."

Song, dance and intention are a potent combination. With Earth Dance, we're realizing the power of music and dance, and it doesn't really matter what tradition or culture you come from—the intention and the resonance are the same across the entire world.

My chanting is my prayer. I draw sound up from a very deep place—it can be likened to dropping a bucket into a deep well and then pulling it back up—when it goes down it's empty and when it reappears it's full! I tap into the silence that is pregnant with sound, but it needs a vehicle to make its sound known. In many ways, I am the container that brings sound into form, and I encourage others to be a vessel, too. The emptier you are, the more sound you can produce.

Sound feeds the soul as water and food feed the body. Through sound we can pour all our longings, frustrations, grief and joys into this mystical container called life, so it can be transformed into a nectar that is sweet and powerful at the same time.

Sound also points to a reality that is a multidimensional, energetic, living and potently filled with unseen beings that are very willing to take form through the repetition and power of the chant. They inform us on an archetypal level of what is possible on this level: sacred power, unconditional love that is imbued with sensuality and aliveness, discriminating wisdom and deep peace, meditation in action and selfless service.

In the process of working sound out of silence, the chant comes into being, permeating our whole energy field, enlivening and transforming the personal as well as the collective. We also become conduits that mediate between earth and sky. We connect the womb of the Earth into the vastness of the sky and glimpse the possibility that we contain both.

I work with chants from every tradition because it allows more people to relate to what I do, and also reveals that they all come from the same source, the same wellspring. This is a devotional practice in that it makes conscious the longing in all of us to be united with the Beloved. At some point, we realize, especially if we chant for long periods of time, that there is no separation between us and the deity or energetics that symbolize the Beloved in our psyche.

The chant allows us a way into the underlying reality that permeates everything, out of which we are constantly dying and being reborn every moment. We are momentarily lifted out of our dual nature, with all its rhetoric, logic and identification, into something vast, timeless and eternal.

The scriptural suggestion "Pray unceasingly" would be a stretch, given that I am not an isolated monk on a mountaintop!

My consciousness, though, does stretch to the mountaintops of higher energies, and my thoughts are steps up and down that ladder of awareness. In this sense, every thought is a prayer, and the universe answers every prayer, whether it is positive or negative.

Therefore, my unceasing prayer is to think positively throughout my day. The form of my prayer might vary according to my level of consciousness at the time.

—When I am in a lower level of consciousness and experience spiritual, emotional, intellectual or physical pain, I ask the Universe for relief.

—When I am at a higher level of consciousness, I manage my affairs with positive, affirmative prayers that direct my day with the Universe.

—When I am at my highest level of consciousness, I surrender and accept the Universe's path for my day:

"How would You have me see this day, be this day, and do this day? Please give this to me with clarity, with the power to carry it out, and with some signs along the way that I am on Your Path. So be it, so it is, and Amen."

The old concept of prayer is often that of someone who is praying for something, like in the Catholic religion, or even offering a penance of a sort in order to get a prayer answered.

It's some kind of wanting, some kind of a deal from God, from life, from the loved one. This old form of prayer is connected with an old way of being somehow in a divided situation: there is the one who wants and someone from whom he can get it—someone outside you who will fulfill your prayer/request.

From the very early age I did not like this concept. Rather, for me, prayer is a state of gratefulness or "prayerfulness," not related to anything or anyone in particular, but a way to feel the connection inside me with the ever-fulfilling state of the divine that is in each of us. Looking at the beauty of a rose, seeing a child playing or the amazing colors of a sunset, hearing the sound of running water; just being here now, in a moment of presence, where you feel one with everything, where there is no more division—that, for me, is living in prayer.

Why would I pray? The pantheist in me says: All is God, all is divine. I am part of all, thus I am divine. There is no separation, no duality, and nothing to pray to. Sometimes this matches my experience; I feel completely at One and in One.

But then there are times when I feel separation. Locked away from communion, I must reach toward the Divine. A prayer is a reaching. My prayer is my practice of breath and movement. Prayer brings me into connection and dissolves separation.

There is a beautiful concept from my spiritual tradition, Sufism, which is "intimate conversation." Spiritual intimacy is a great tenderness, a feeling of warmth, a whispering quality of enlivened joy ringing in my heart and cells. This fills me. I feel greatly small, as small as a cell or even smaller, and delicate yet indestructible. I become a tiny vibration. The conversation is heart to heart, cell to cell.

Sometimes spiritual intimacy describes the quiet presence shared with others. Sometimes spiritual intimacy is the sensation within my own body. Sometimes spiritual intimacy is the unwinding of my cells and a stirring of my me-ness into the Beyond.

My flesh is all prayer.
It moves me into Communion.
When my breath clears the haze of thoughts,
when my feet tamp down,
when my bones write along the skins of space,
my organs and blood read the volumes beyond me.
Those big prayers.

"Let the beauty we love be what we do. There are hundreds of ways to kneel and kiss the ground."

Rumi
Translated by Coleman Barks

There are so many ways to kneel and worship, as the good poet-saint sings. Who can limit this radiant, buoyant spirit? When I feel agitated or overwhelmed, or simply don't know what to do, I just put my head down and join my hands together before my breast and pray. It's almost always wordless, as I simply don't know what to do or ask for, or where to turn except deeper in order to center myself. This kind of stopping and dropping (everything) into wordless, agenda-free, humble and simple speechless prayer has tremendous power, and I can't extol it enough. "Absolutely unmixed attention is prayer," says French mystic Simone Weil.

Here is the vital heart of the matter: In the Tibetan language, the word for prayer is *monlam*, literally meaning "aspiration-path." Prayer power has much to do with intention, resolve and motivation, focus and clarity, as well as to whom we may be praying to and what for. All languages are understood in prayer, for the prayerful heart has the gift of tongues in which no translation is necessary. It's better to have a heart without words than words without a heart, so put your heart and soul into what you're doing, saying and praying and all will be accomplished. Everything depends upon intention and motivation. I've heard that prayer is how we talk to God and/or a universal higher power, and meditation is how we listen. A prayerful heart is an open heart. Singing is believing; sacred music and chant can provide both an ecstatic experience and directly connect one to a higher power or Oneness that is transcendent over any of us yet immanent in all of us.

I was taught very early in my life that: "A heart without prayer is better than a prayer without heart."

I was also taught by my grandfather, Mohandas K. Gandhi, that the best form of prayer is service of the poor. Gandhi's outlook on religion was unique. He would say that religion is like climbing a mountain and striving to get to the peak, so why should it matter to anyone which side of the mountain one chooses to climb up from? The combination of all these unique experiences taught me to respect all religions as I respect my own: Hinduism. To show respect to all religions, I incorporate prayers from all the major religions of the world when I sit down to pray.

Sometimes my prayer takes the form of service of the poor in a constructive way. I don't mean just feeding the poor and making them dependent, but helping them rebuild their self-respect and self-confidence so that they can stand on their own feet and fend for themselves.

I am called many things: Elder; African American; woman; Dharma teacher; author; lesbian; student of wisdom traditions; world traveler; daughter in a family of eight raised in South Central Los Angeles, by a single mom from a working-class, churchgoing family during the Civil Rights Movement; a mom at age 15; a homeowner at 21; an open-heart surgery patient at 27. I'm all these things and more—*and* I'm none of these things. I've been one self that has taken on many forms over multiple lifetimes to respond to what's forgotten, denied, and unhealed in the world.

For over twenty years, my prayer practice has been Theravada Buddhism. This tradition offers mindfulness meditation as its foundation, which teaches you how to be free from suffering by recognizing the nature of existence and cultivating a peaceful relationship with your thoughts, feelings and actions. My attraction to this tradition came much later in life, after I had explored many other spiritual traditions in many parts of the world.

Buddhism was appealing because it mirrored how I'd come to understand myself as a spiritual being. It didn't promise perfection or salvation. Instead, the teachings and the practice put the fate of my freedom in my own hands. The Buddha teaches: *Don't take my word for it; see for yourself.* This is key because my daily practice proves that I know what I can only know for myself.

Mindfulness meditation helps me cultivate a basis for how I both view and experience the meaning of life, living and death. When I meditate, I am teaching my mind to ride the energies of my intense emotions and to become aware of what I need to heal from the inside out. I am learning how to stay present, and I am growing in my awareness that the present moment is worth living fully and without elaboration, and how each letting go, each exhale is a death.

While I have a daily sitting practice, I pray continuously—on and off the cushion—walking, standing, eating and sleeping; in breathing, speech, thought and action. When I pray, I am not requesting help from a higher power. Praying is a gentle and ongoing reminder for myself to live in alignment with my highest intentions: respect for life, true contentment, pure love, caring speech, deep listening and wholesome nourishment and healing. I believe that all beings, without exception, benefit from my practice. This includes enemies, strangers, teachers, elders, children, loved ones, all sentient beings and the planet. The Buddha shares these intentions.

Prayer is the act of loving awareness—a noble presence—and you don't ignore, reject or over-identify with what is revealing itself. In mindfulness meditation, I am able to stay close to the truth of the moment without the suffering of the moment. I can notice, for instance, that awareness of anger is not angry, and awareness of fear is not frightened. Awareness is simply aware and is not attached to the story I add to the situation. Most additions to the story contribute to and prolong suffering.

When I feel perplexed by the sorrows throughout the world and how Earth is suffering because of our greed, hatred and ignorance, I pray not so much to fix the problems but to wake up the minds of those who are ignorant of how they contribute to the suffering in the world. I ask that I, too, wake up to my own ignorance. I pray with my breath by inhaling the difficulty and exhaling peace. This prayer practice may happen several times within any given hour and throughout the day. My prayer mantra is: *May all beings be safe from inner and outer harm, happy and content, healthy and strong, and live with ease.*

My mindfulness practice has been good medicine for my heart and mind, and for living with good intention. It also challenges me to embody my spiritual practice by serving in ways that nourish the planet and touch, shape and heal the global human heart.

From the time I was three years old I was questioning whether there was a God. I remember once, when I was around eight years old, locking myself in the bathroom. I said, "If you exist, I need a sign. Anything at all." I listened and looked. I only saw darkness and heard silence. The longer I listened, the deeper I fell into the dark silence. After a while I came back and felt that I had not received any sign at all, and while this was not a sign that God did not exist, I could not know if there was a God or not. Religion seemed pointless to me. It all seemed fake. So while I would mouth the prayers as long as I was required to attend synagogue, I never prayed.

The first time I ever remember praying was when I was a federal fugitive. I had freed a prisoner and knocked down two police officers during the May Day protests against the Vietnam War in 1971. After being released on bail from a maximum security jail, with two charges of assault on a federal police officer, I did not appear for my grand jury indictment, and a federal warrant was issued for my arrest.

Three months later I was arrested in Denver during a marijuana bust. I was in the city jail for a few days as they ran checks on me. They found an FBI report on my political activities in Denver so they kept me as long as they could.

I prayed for help. I didn't know if there was a God or not. I didn't believe in God but if help was available, I was praying for it. Miraculously or coincidentally, my prayer was answered.

Those were the pre-computer days, and I had used an alias in the Washington, D.C., arrest, so my federal fugitive warrant was not discovered. The police let me out on bail. I ended up—after facing over 40 years in prison for all charges—getting out of it all. I never had to spend any real time in jail.

That was my first prayer that I can remember, and it worked. It was a prayer for help. It seems that most prayers are prayers for help, either for me personally or for someone else that I know, or prayers of thanks or worship.

I don't pray for help now. I would say my life is a prayer of gratitude.

I can't say it happens every time, but almost always, I wake up with a prayer of gratitude alive in my heart. I wake up smiling inside and out. I am grateful for everything.

I have been grateful for the Goddess ever since my release from jail, as that is what I named the force that I sensed around me at that time. Before meeting my teacher, Papaji, in 1990, I met the Goddess in 1975. The Goddess came to me in a human form of my life partner, Gangaji. I am married to the Goddess. How could I be more lucky, how could I be more grateful?

At this stage of my life, I have a terminal, incurable blood cancer called multiple melanoma. This rare type of leukemia has the effect of dissolving one's bones. When it was discovered, I had a broken back. I had been doing everything I knew to deal with the pain in my back for almost eight months. I tried acupuncture, massage and herbs, but everything seemed to make it worse. A year earlier I had vowed to carry the pain of the suffering I had caused in my personal relationships in my bones forever, and that is what I thought I was dealing with. After spending most of each day in bed and in pain for months, I was finally convinced to get an MRI. My surgeon said the MRI showed the spine of an osteoporotic eighty-year-old woman with lesions from the top of my head to my chest. A biopsy done during an operation to "glue" back together my fractured spine showed the cancer.

By the time I got to treatment at the Myeloma Institute, the cancer had been dissolving my bones for about eight months. The cancer doctors said this cancer can be smoldering or it can be like fire, and I've got a ten-alarm fire. The cancer was at stage three. I also had the highest cancer counts that some of the doctors in the institute had seen. Statistically speaking, two-thirds of myeloma patients are dead within three years of the cancer's onset, so I was facing death. But this circumstance did not touch my gratitude. My prayer of gratitude is deeper than circumstances, good or bad. I was ready to die and ready to live, with no preference. I only wanted my life or my death to be in the best service of this grace.

I wanted my life to be well used, and it is well used. I am fulfilled, live or die. I wanted my death to be well used too. If it means dying in this moment, I am grateful—and if it means living past this moment, I am also grateful.

Gangaji and I had a visit with Ram Dass recently. We went to thank him for being an older brother on the path. We have different gurus but we celebrated together the divine love, the divine gratitude and the fruit of living at the guru's feet. We celebrated the grace that has entered our lives.

Gratitude has been my prayer since meeting my teacher in 1990. That meeting with the fire of liberation was the culmination of my life. I met someone who passed on the fire of silence and the liberation of consciousness into the realization of its true nature. For this, I am forever grateful and my prayer is to give back this life to that which set it free.

Prayer is gratefulness and gratitude. Different teachers, different paths, same love, same devotion, same gratitude.

I used to contract when someone would speak too often and evangelically of God, harkening back to my teens when it was a prelude to someone wanting to save my everlasting soul. For that reason, I abandoned church, and with it, prayer. Coming home to Spirit has been a process spanning decades, until finally I came to the point when I realized sometimes those who talk enthusiastically about God may have something really wonderful to share. And I don't want to miss it!

That was the day I prayed, my way, for a way to reframe the word God. My way is to feel my feet firmly on the sacred Earth, so I can breathe that energy up through my body until it reaches my heart. Then I extend that Earth energy up through the rest of my body, out the crown of my head, and extend my arms up and out around me to open my personal sacred space where I call in the Great Spirit, my guides, ancestors, helping allies and angels. Asking from that perspective, the answer came in an instant: God is G—O—D, Great Open Door, the gateway to the vastness and generosity of the Universe, All That Is.

Prayer, to me, is the recognition that Spirit is not going to intervene unless I ask. I can move through life on my own, hoping for the best, or I can ASK for support and guidance. I can commune daily and learn how Spirit speaks to me, which is often through automatic writing, and then I know how to listen in those moments when I am overwhelmed or facing a crisis. I have learned to trust what I hear in those split seconds when I am challenged to act.

Prayer won't stop the inevitable cycles of loss and death and pain inherent in the human condition. But because it has become a practice that enriches my life, it opens me to grace in times of grief and a place to surrender when there is absolutely no way I can figure things out. (I still usually try to work it out myself first, characteristic of the human condition!) God is, to me, the Great Mystery. And prayer is the way to connect with All That Is.

Never before have I been so vulnerable. My life hangs by a thin thread—each and every heartbeat is a gift of Grace, which might cease at any moment. I could die at any moment—literally.

"We live not by the breath that flows in and out, but by the One who makes the breath flow in and out." (Katha Upanishad) I live not by the heart that beats from moment to moment, but by the One who makes the heart beat from moment to moment—or doesn't, and I die.

The above excerpt comes from my personal journal the day after I received—out of the blue—a life-threatening diagnosis in 2001. The doctors told me I was perfectly healthy, except that I might drop dead at any moment from sudden cardiac arrest, due to a heart arrhythmia. What a bizarre shock! They scheduled me for surgery the following Monday to implant a defibrillator, and sent me home for the weekend with instructions to come to the emergency room immediately if I had symptoms lasting more than four seconds.

I was plunged into inner chaos, terror, supreme peace, total surrender—and everything in between. Four times over those next two days my heart stopped momentarily, and I did not know whether it would start up again. Silent prayer and non-dual meditation practice had taken me to unspeakable depths, heights, humbling and grace over the years, but nothing had prepared me for this. The journal entry continues:

My heart is broken. Deeply and literally. You have broken it open, Lord, and now it can only function by your grace. You dangle me at the cliff edge of life and death. You choose, moment to moment, whether to keep this heart going, or to end this life.

Oh death!—become my friend! For you surround me now—whirling all around me like a great dark cloud—ready to swallow me whole at any moment.

Forgive me, Oh Lord! This was always, ever true! But now it is so starkly revealed.

"Abandon all supports, take refuge in Me alone!" So why would I entrust my life to an electro-mechanical device? Oh Lord, if I pray deeply enough, won't You be my defibrillator? And if You did not save my life, then wouldn't that be your will? And if the defibrillator shocks me back into life, am I then living against Your will?

I beg for Your answer!

I heard simply, "Do the procedure."

Kill me—take it all! I dedicate this body, this life—and all its suffering to You. I want You, oh supreme Lord, and you alone. Let this ordeal be an offering to you. Take me!—on your terms—and do what you will. But do not deny me union with you!—I beg you!

Years of meditation practice proved to be extremely helpful on one level and entirely useless on another. I spent hours on the cushion those two days, and it was a wild ride—at times incredible terror, grief, anguish that literally vibrated throughout my being, powerful experiences of cleansing and forgiveness, and several sustained periods of indescribable peace and profound acceptance of whatever was to be. Long-cultivated sitting practices of non-dual awareness were basically cast aside, replaced by intensive prayer in a naked, desperate plea with the Absolute—for my life. The journal entry continues, though the words do not do justice to the experience:

Dear God, I feel such fear going into this. "Give it to Me," I heard a voice say. Oh Lord, I give all my fear and terror to You.

Dear Lord, if it be your will, I ask that I might live. Not for my various projects, which all seem so trite! If it be Your will, let me live so that the spiritual work You have begun through this form can be completed. I have realized the true purpose of life. If it be Thy will, allow this purpose to be fulfilled.

Oh Lord, I want You alone!—come what may. This body is not my body, it is your body. You created this body and lent it to my soul; you have the right to do with it what you will.

Let it be as You, not I, would have it.

I have many prayers. Most important to me is my life, which I consider to be a moving prayer. I try and bring consciousness to all of my choices to help increase the flow of love on the planet. I also pray to various aspects of God, never hesitating to ask for help, or to volunteer it. Lastly, I frequently pray that I be shown what I need in order to change.

Through most of my life, I don't think I really understood prayer. God was a figure of speech to me and my upbringing was really about individualism. My mother was a follower of Ayn Rand and Idra Devi—very contrasting belief systems swirled around my mother's core. We talked about affirmations and meditations and we built altars from nature. The word "prayer" was brought to those beautiful altars she built with me. In a way, it was more about aesthetics and confirmation than anything. As I got older, this stimulated a metaphysical, spiritual imprint. God, to me, was equated with the Big Bang, simplicity, beauty, nature and creation. It was an abstract concept. I accepted simplicity going into complexity, which is exactly how my childhood seemed to develop. It was so simple and pure, and there was an endowment of temperament. That changed because of conditions.

In 1999 one of my children was in a terrible car accident. He was hanging by a thread. When I arrived at the hospital where he was in intensive care, I stopped in the chapel before going to his bedside. I begged for God to allow my child to live, and I promised I would stay linked with the source of God, a power greater than me, if he would only save my boy. He was left a paraplegic after his accident. I'm not sure if God is male or female, but I am linked with God, because I made a commitment. Although my spiritual and moral discipline is to Buddhism, God reigns supreme over all. I did not know that in giving me the life of my son, whose name happens to be Xavier (meaning bright, or splendid), that this was preparation for me to lose my oldest child seven years later. Tessa, who was in the Peace Corps, was killed in a shark attack on February 1, 2006. When the director of this organization phoned me with the tragic news, in those first few seconds, all I could think was "There is no God!" Then I remembered the promise, the commitment, the deal I had placed when the Source had given me Xavier's life. Tessa's death, her loss, opened up great accomplishment, not only for me, but for her father, her siblings and her extended family.

I pray every day for our biggest resource: the young people of the world. They are the new democracy, which will carry us into many generations of prayer and hopefulness.

Blessings, my friend—be happy, healthy and holy while you pray.

I find that the moments when we most need to be connected to a force and field of life greater than ourselves, are the very ones when we are apt to shut down and withhold prayer. As we often forget to breathe in a time of disappointment and despair, so too do we forget to pray, as if to say to God, "If you are not going to play on my terms, then I am just going to take all of my marbles and go home," refusing to accept life on its own terms.

The holiest moments of our lives are when we make the choice to turn towards life, rather than away, in the face of all of life's toppling and shocking losses. To say a prayer that aligns us with all that is good, loving, beautiful and true in the midst of the rubble and the despair, and rather than ask God to make this better for us, to declare instead who we will be in the face of it.

It is in this sacred instant that we awaken to ourselves as the generators of life and love, and begin to understand prayer as the holy act of co-creation.

For much of my professional life, I have worked as an anthropologist and worshiped solely at the altar of science. Then, in July of 2003, I was taken to a place of great power on the side of the most sacred mountain in Polynesia, the volcano Mauna Kea in the center of Hawai'i Island. I was in the company of a revered Hawaiian elder and chief named Hale Kealohalani Makua, who was a well-known kahuna mystic. Half a head taller than me, with a long white ponytail down his back and a white bushy beard framing his dark face, Chief Makua had considerable presence.

On that day, we walked together up the rocky incline among scrubby trees and bushes at the 9,000-foot level, the chief leaning heavily on his carved walking stick. When we achieved the ridge directly above us, we found ourselves on the rim of an almost perfect circular crater, much like a steep bowl, more than a hundred yards across and several hundred feet deep. This place, Makua told me, was called Ha'i Wahine—Speaking Woman.

It was mid-morning. The chief's eyes ranged outward and his lips whispered a longish prayer in Hawaiian. Above us, the mountain rose in all its magnificence to almost 14,000 feet. Before us, the unimaginable blue mass of its sister mountain loomed above us to the south, the volcano Mauna Loa of almost equal height. Makua had brought me to this place to encounter a mountain spirit.

The chief finished his prayer, then glanced at me. "What you now need to do is this: First you must walk the circumference of this crater rim three times," gesturing to his right. He smiled. "Then I will tell you what comes next."

I knew that Makua was interested to see how Nature would respond to me. He watched speculatively as I considered the landscape around us. There was no trail to follow, but I set off along the crater rim. I hadn't gone far when, without warning, a most amazing thing happened. As I walked along the ridge, picking my way carefully between the stones, I began to pray. It was as though

I had passed into some "prayer field," for lack of a better term, and almost immediately, I was praying hard.

I prayed for myself and for my family, for Makua and for his family, for the ancestors and for the spirits, and for all of humanity who seemed to have lost their way. I prayed for our often-misguided administration in Washington, and for the leadership at all levels of human society, everywhere, and I prayed for all the peoples of the world. And as I prayed, I walked, and each intake and out-breath of air through my lungs was a prayer.

Throughout, my scientist's mind was taking this all in. I had never engaged in prayer at this level before, yet prayer, I reasoned, was a way of talking to the gods and to the spirit of this place. Perhaps I had wandered into an energetic "prayer zone" that had been established here long before my time. I wondered if this was part of Nature's response.

When I approached the chief at the end of my first circuit, he was watching me with interest. "You see that stone over there?" he asked me, pointing to his right. There, on the rocky substrate, was a small lava bomb about the size and shape of an American football and pointed at both ends. The stone's curious layering gave it the appearance of having eyes. "I was sitting here watching you circumnavigating the rim, and that stone spoke to me," the chief told me. "It said, 'Hey... who's that guy?' So I replied, 'And who are you?' We then had an interesting conversation in which I told the stone who you are. That stone then said to me 'Oh!'"

Makua watched me as I looked at the stone carefully. "The stone said that you don't have to walk around again...that you're ready to go down into the crater. And as you do, you must pray... you must pray to the spirit that resides here, and in your prayer, you must offer her your aloha and state your intentions for being in this place. And then, if she is so inclined," he grinned, "she will respond."

Allow me to say in all humility that when I emerged from the crater a couple of hours later, I was somewhat mind-blown, for the spirit did respond ... and with great love. Makua looked me over with satisfaction. My life has never been quite the same, and every breath ... and every moment of every day ... is now a prayer.

The chief then shared this thought with me: "Know that when you offer prayer, you find love within its pure form, and you are no longer finite. In those moments, you have found your eternity. When we are able to let our love free to ride the wind of spirit, and this is our breath that carries our prayers, we are now following the blueprint we have laid out for our own growth. And it is precisely then that we may choose how we shall serve that mystery that created us and all that is..."

I have always been grateful for the gift of life, which I express through words of gratitude.

My prayers have always started by giving thanks to our Creator for our gifts: music, dance, life, food, shelter, love, family, plants, medicines, waters, birds, trees, fruits, crops, tobacco, food, clothing, animals, thunder beings, our Mother Earth and her generosity...

Among the Iroquois, every day is one of thanksgiving.

My prayers are directed to a higher spirit. I ask the Creator to give me the songs that will bring messages of peace, hope and love to the world.

My personal ritual begins where I open myself up to the Creator: I then address my ancestors and spirit guides to direct me, and let the music flow.

Once, an Inuit elder waited long after a performance to talk to me. She said that she was told that songs would be carried across the ice from the birds through the ancestors to those who would bring the songs to the people. She said when she heard me sing, the music of the ancient ones was being brought forward through the birds' songs and I was one of those chosen to carry them along. My own grandmother used to call me her little "songbird." I felt so blessed.

I believe prayer is connecting with one's inner soul to the universal power of creation.

Praying, to me, is not asking or wishing but putting myself into a place of "being," where I can open my heart and soul and accept and welcome the gift of the ancient beauty of music.

medicine buddha © lama gyurme

gina rose halpern

Art is prayer made visible
Music is prayer made audible
Dance is prayer embodied
But the greatest art we practice
Is the art of Compassion
Which is prayer in action and service.

Prayer is chanting in the Great Pyramid, kneeling in the Blue Mosque, and touching the damp earth of the moon temple in Macchu Picchu.

I pray through my breath, as my breath filters through thoughts while surrendering to the divine.

Prayer is connecting with the Earth's benevolent, life-giving frequencies through the bottom of my feet.

Prayer is the butterfly that moves through me with the synchronicity of life, morphing changing, emerging.

Prayer is shed through my tears, my laughter and through the clenching of my jaws.

Prayer is all of life, the everlasting flow of utmost bliss.

Prayer is an urgent 911 call, the dawning of a new day and the setting of the sun and moon.

Prayer is attunement with a bee communing with the nectar of a flower.

Prayer is consciousness, awareness, the present moment.

When I pray I embody truth, wisdom and peace while unleashing what is not.

I am that, I am as prayer, through prayer connecting to the heartbeat of all that is.

I pray to restore my connection to God, to the Universe, to All There Is. I use prayer to begin my day, to call in my ancestors and pray for guidance and protection. It lifts me and aligns my auric fields in the highest frequency possible.

To pray this way, sit comfortably in your chair and feel your spine as a flexible, moving chain. Relax your shoulders. Feel your neck rise upward from the shoulders and your head balanced freely. Take a deep breath, and let go of all the thoughts, ideas and hopes you have connected to the outcome of this day. You have arrived at the right place at the right time. There is nothing more to run for, nothing more to achieve—this is just one moment for you to connect to your soul.

Listen to the sounds of the room and then to the sounds of the building beyond. Listen with your heart, farther out to the sounds of the spheres, the ethers, the big harmony, the great OM. Every cell in your body resonates with that very same frequency and rhythm and vibrates in the cosmic dance of all that is. Now fall into the stillness deep within, where the sound falls silent and time and space cease to be, and eternity holds you.

In this place, you are your Divine self, the Divine spark, and you can never be hurt or harmed. You are always in the perfection of the Creator. You are unconditional love...an eternal being.

Call forth all of your ancestors to be with you so you can hear their songs of their joys and accomplishments, their failures, guilt and suffering. Come into an exchange of blessings and love, so they can heal and you can heal. Call forth all the Beings of the Light, your guardian angels and guides and the masters of the ascended realms, asking for their guidance, love and protection so that only the highest good for everybody can happen here and now.

When you are ready, say the following: "With this, I am perfectly prepared to begin with my work of the day."

Move your fingers and toes, breathe fully and give your body a good stretch.

Recently, I imagined my father waking me in the middle of the night in my childhood room with a delighted smile and the words: *Wake up and pray!* That never happened. The thought came from my decade-long study of the life of Fatima, the daughter of the Prophet Muhammad, for a book I'm writing. She experienced this wake-and-pray message from her father more than once. I have considered those startling late-night words from a great man of prayer. It feels to me that he is saying: *Stay awake, be connected to the Spirit of Guidance at all times!*

Sometimes prayer seems as if it is under clay and will not release. When that happens, my tool to penetrate the hard ground is gratitude. Breathing out gratitude and breathing in gratitude loosens the cramped places, with their focus on me, just me. Gratitude opens into clear transparencies, connecting my heart and the Oneness through the masters, saints and prophets, so prayers can begin to flow.

May I serve the message of love, harmony and beauty. May I have the health and clarity to be of benefit to self and others! May the people I mention in these prayers be well, safe and happy. May those struggling in despair each heal from his or her illness and/or pain. May ALL be well, safe and happy.

In my prayer, I hold each warring country like a baby. I hum a lullaby to Syria, having stayed there and seen her face. A friend told me that when he recognizes despair or anger, he claims it and moves into physical exercise as a kind of body prayer—there is a shift that gives him energy.

Prayer is a responsibility. I make the intention to cultivate peace and harmony through daily meditation. *May I stay awake, be connected to the Spirit of Guidance at all times!*

Everyone in the world should be able to sleep without fear, at least for one night.

Everyone should be able to eat to his fill, at least for one day.

There should be at least one day when hospitals see no one admitted due to violence.

By doing selfless service for at least one day, everyone should help the poor and needy.

It is Amma's prayer that at least this small dream be realized.

I pray in many different ways.

Before going up onto a mountain to fast and pray on a vision quest, or before entering a sweat lodge, I pray in a traditional, Native American way, by making sacred prayer ties and offering them with heart and intention to the Great Spirit.

Each prayer tie contains a small amount of tobacco, wrapped in a colored cloth, tied in sequence with a string. Each represents a calling for guidance or help—for myself or others—or an expression of gratitude for the blessings in my life, or an offering of surrender to the great unknown.

Most often, though, I simply go into nature alone, or into my meditation room, sit quietly, turn my attention inward, let go of the outer world, and listen as deeply as I can to the voices of Spirit whispering inside.

In my prayers, I seek to understand and embrace the totality of All That Is, including the spirit of love, the light of God and the radiant divine essence—as well as the darkness, the shadows of existence and the pain and suffering within myself and within all of humanity. I pray for the strength and courage to hold—with tenderness, compassion, humility and grace—*all* of the opposites that appear within myself and in the world; to forgive myself and others; and to rest in the gentle, silent awareness—and the spirit of freedom, wholeness and love—that lie within the heart of all beings.

I'm Lakota from Hasapa, the Black Hills in South Dakota—the heart of Mother Earth. We have a word for prayer: *Chekia*. *Che* is to cry. *Kia* is to send your voice out to the Creator, Wankan Tanka, the Great Spirit.

We, the people of Turtle Island (North America), have an understanding: Mother Earth has a heart, and it's what our ceremonies are about. A film image of the Black Hills, taken via satellite and fast-forwarded through the four seasons, looks like a heart that is pumping.

The word *Che* is about what brought the people down to their knees. The people had nothing left but prayer. And prayer has to come from the heart. We were told that everything we send from the heart is good. And the people say that mind, body, and spirit are connected to the heart. The Creator gave us a mind to make good decisions or bad decisions. The Creator said that the heart's drum—the heartbeat—is ongoing life, and the heart is where we utilize and recognize everything, where we realize that we have certain things to work with as a human being.

We walk upon Mother Earth. We pray for all things to be good because our Creator gave us the understanding that all ceremony has to be of purity. So the White Buffalo Calf Woman gave us instructions to do our ceremonies in that manner, to walk in a sacred manner, and to give thanks or *wopala*—no matter how bad things are or how good things are, we still have to give *wopala*, to be humble under the Creator all the time.

There's a moon—a full moon with an Indian in it, and the Indian sits cross-legged and has his head down with two feathers hanging down to remind us we have to stay humble under the Creator, Wankan Tanka, the Great Spirit. Prayer is a very sacred time that all of us have to go through, each individual has to be in that humble place to send our voice to Wakan Tanka, the Great Spirit.

You have to feel that prayer, and be sincere. It's like going on a vision quest and coming to that place where you give yourself to the Creator because you have an understanding that this is what life is about. That's when the Creator hears your voice and answers your prayers—when you're in that humble place, either on the hill or at home. When you are sincere and your heart is really mean, it's hurting and you are crying for help. That's where the word *Chekia* comes from. *Chekia* is a sacred word to us.

We have to take care of everything about life. That's why we say *Mitakuye Oyasin*, which means that everything is related: the two-legged, the four-legged, the winged ones, the ones that swim and crawl. Because we have boundaries, we follow the animal nation, because they too live upon Mother Earth and the Creator, the Great Spirit. That's why we give tobacco every time we go after our medicine. That plant has to be a live medicine. The Sundance Tree has to be a live Sundance Tree, and the buffalo has to be a live buffalo to use in ceremony because it gave its life for us to live.

So we have that tobacco, and we pray from our hearts—*Chekia*—to the Grandfathers, to the Four Winds, to the Great Spirit, to Mother Earth. And this is how much we understand: That life is a cycle and no one person is higher than the other. We stand in a circle when we do a prayer because life has no ending and it has no beginning. The purpose of the life that we live upon the Earth is to take care of Spirit, and when a person comes here it is a gift.

When a child is born, when a child comes here, we pray from our hearts—*Chekia*. We send our voices to the Great Spirit and give thanks. The mother and father have to be there and the mother has to love this baby, to pray from her heart—*Chekia*—to have that child, to nurse that baby in that ceremony. And the father has to bury that afterbirth. No matter where that child grows up and goes—to the four different winds and to travel—when a person dies, they have to be buried near that afterbirth **because** that's our territory. So from the time that child is born, we raise that child to understand *Chekia* until that child goes into the spirit world.

Chekia is the last word, the last prayer that we have for the one whose life is done here on the face of the Earth, to send that person on to the Wankan Tanka. So the word *Chekia* is important until the time we are done here on Mother Earth.

So that's one of the first words that Great Spirit gave us—the word *Chekia*, to pray.

Aho.

Prayer to me is anything we do that opens our heart, mind and soul to the always-with-us presence of Sacred Cosmic Mystery Creator with the intention to give thanks for gifts of grace in our lives. And in connecting with the infinite light and love of Spirit, we are asking to be used as a channel for those gifts into the world, sending God/Goddess Love into others without attachment to a result.

One of my daily prayers is:

Thank you, Great Spirit, for the Sacred Gift of the Life Force, for the Sacred Gifts of Creation, and for Your Presence Here, Now and Always. Thank you for Ancestors, Family, Marriage, Community and Friends. Thank you for light, love, health, peace, wisdom, protection, financial success and abundance. I pray for Peace in our Hearts, Peace in the world, Peace for All People and for a Healthy Sacred Hoop of Life. May All Beings Live with peace, freedom and justice, in light, love and wisdom, with food, clothing, shelter, health care, education and meaningful, gainful employment opportunities, living together as respectful sisters and brothers, relatives of one family, in sustainable harmony and balance with all of Creation. May it be so, and with your help, may I show up to do my part to live fully, to love fully and make a positive difference by knowing you, loving you and serving you. Aho.

How I pray: like this. I am praying right now. Writing, for me, is prayer. Dipping deep into the wellspring of my own secret heart, reaching and pausing and listening for the voice of the mystery and inviting it to speak through me, stringing together luminous words in hopes of offering something of beauty. Before I write, I light a candle and invoke the saints and prophets, the angels and ancestors, and the great limitless emptiness that is plenitude. In this way, writing writes me, and prayer prays me.

I remember in the mid-1970s, when I was around sixteen and living on my own in northern California, a friend took me to the Bay Area to meet Zalman Schachter-Shalomi, a rabbi he had begun studying with. Although I was born Jewish, my family had traded in organized religion for a more organic version of spirituality, and I was suspicious of the God of my ancestors. A small group had coalesced around this man, Reb Zalman, and the ecstatic, inclusive quality of his teachings. I spent the weekend in their company. There was a lot of talk about prayer and a lot of praying in Hebrew, English, even Arabic. I hung back and watched, listened, trying to maintain my skepticism; yet, I was magnetically drawn to the deep quiet I sensed at the heart of all the poetic words and haunting melodies.

On the last night, as I lay in my sleeping bag, I decided to try it. "Um, God?" I whispered. "I don't know how to do this. Could you please show me?" The response was instantaneous. A state of prayer flooded my being like morning light through flung-open curtains. There was no personified being standing at the foot of my bed, poised for conversation. All forms fell away, language melted, concepts dissolved, and I became prayer. "Oh," I said. "Just this."

So there is something about stepping lightly aside and allowing the grace of the present moment to fill the empty cup of the heart. This happens when I write about the teachings of the mystics and when I'm chopping vegetables and sliding them into a hot wok. It can happen when I sit on my black cushion in the mornings and count my breaths and when I'm kissing the tear-streaked face of a child. This is prayer. It is non-dual and yet deeply devotional. It is the momentary merging of the lover that I am into the Beloved that God is, so that all that is left is love.

I am a 70-year-old Franciscan priest, and my prayer life parallels my human life. As a young person I talked trustfully to a God who was *out there*—but at least good, and could be cajoled by right words and good behavior (and also hurt and lost by bad behavior). But the imagined and hoped-for relationship was at least established. It was probably the way I humanly loved and related at that time.

Then, in the middle of life I began, step by step, largely through failure, to recognize an inner Vitality and Source that I learned to trust and rely upon even more. Each new step was a falling into mercy that was both given to me and yet was also *from me!* How could this be? Incarnation became so real.

In late middle age, this "spring inside me" began "welling up" (John 4:14), and I knew it was not me but a Presence that was Life Itself. I was merely a happy participant. Others were drawing from the same well and also pouring into it.

Now I just wake, and breathe, and I sometimes speak words to bring the water to the surface—for others who do not know their own depths, for me to know my own soul, and for the always remote One to whom I am speaking (God has to remain mysterious to keep me searching and humble, and to protect my own human position, which naked Divinity would overwhelm).

My prayer is both within and without now, to "this One in whom I live, and move, and have my very being" (Acts 17:28).

In whatever I am doing, I ask for Spirit to work through me. Every moment becomes a prayer: following inspirations and calls; connecting with nature, the inner world, and the beauty of peoples' unique gifts; allowing myself to be guided; staying present and persevering through the obstacles that inevitably occur; being rewarded with a bounty of unexpected images, inspirations and experiences. As I integrate them, they make connections, catalyze and open doors for others. I rarely have any idea when I am embarking of what will unfold or how spirit will come through, but my prayer, faith and experience is that it always does.

This is the amazing grace of prayer.

light being, 1992 susan slotter

I really wanted to make films. Movies that matter.

I enrolled in a unique documentary film program with a social issue and ethnographic slant. The climax was the exercise where you got to make a fifteen-minute film. If I got that right, I could parlay my sample reel into the movie.

The exercise came out well. Sample reel in hand, I was ready to make the movie. But how do you get the money? They never taught us that.

I was clueless. Then I realized I knew one person who'd founded a hospice and must have raised money to do it. At lunch, I popped the question. She looked at me quizzically. After a long pause, she looked me deep in my eye and asked, "Have you tried prayer?"

You must be kidding, I thought.

Over the coming weeks, no great insights or epiphanies shone on me. Sheepishly, I decided to give prayer a chance.

The household in which I grew up was adamantly secular. My parents escaped the Brooklyn Jewish 'hood when my father achieved the grail of moving uptown to become an Ivy League professor at Columbia. They were elated to be liberated from the Old World of religious superstition and magical thinking. My mother was and is a militant atheist. Ethics, values, service—you bet. But spirituality was a four-letter word in our home. Spirituality, schmirituality.

I had no idea how to pray. I'd dabbled with yoga and meditation for a few years, so I figured I'd try sitting and see what happened.

Gradually something did happen. I realized I was on fire to make this film, and I believed it was important.

Then I ran up against a barrier. Myself. I could feel I was not wired to receive the support I needed. Like most of us in this culture, I am far better at giving than receiving. So I began rewiring myself to receive the support I felt the project and I deserved.

I asked around if any of my friends knew potential funders. The second funder I pitched said "yes." It was a small amount of money, about $200, but it was a green light and it came with enthusiasm. Approximately the next ten people said "no," but it was too late. That fatal first money hooks you and there's no turning back.

But still, prayer was a dubious proposition to me. I couldn't help feeling cheesy about asking for things for myself. In the taxonomy of prayer, that's called intercessory prayer. It struck me as a tawdry Santa's List hitched to the peculiarly American Gospel of Wealth. I decided it was not really about me, but for a higher purpose.

I found a similar problem with visualizing exactly what you want, a la *The Secret*. The cosmos is so inconceivably complex and vastly more intelligent than you or me that it's laughably limiting to get too specific about what you might think you want. Best to go for top-line intention and leave the details to the big wheels of cosmic forces.

When I invited Chief Oren Lyons, an elder from the Iroquois Six Nations, to speak about prayer at the Bioneers conference, he showed bemused consternation. In Iroquois spirituality, he said, there's not really such a thing as prayer. What we call prayer is, for his people, a daily consciousness, a ritualized way of relationship, a state of constant gratitude expressed in countless ceremonies and a way of life.

Sure, sometimes I pray for things I want or need—I'm no angel. I'm more comfortable setting intentions and seeking guidance toward the greater good—as murky, subjective and delusional as that can be. Intention counts for a lot in this world of Intention Deficit Disorder.

But hey, what do I know? These days, I try to attune my heart to receive with grace whatever the cosmos has up its sleeve. Maybe pray for rain. Give thanks. Hang out in the mystery.

Spiritual, schmiritual.

I am often asked (as are many atheists and agnostics, I am sure), "But without religion, without a belief in God, how can you find meaning in life—have you no spirituality?"

One can admire and feel reverent toward the awesome powers of nature, the amazing way in which life reproduces itself, the sheer immensity of time and space, without necessarily imagining that there is "somebody" running it all. It is amazing. It is immense. It is almost beyond human comprehension—although, little by little, we humans are beginning to understand something about how it works (thanks to science, by the way, and not to religion!).

I live on a large piece of land. We have our own forests, hills, meadows, trails and roads, located in an area of Oregon where the climate is very mild. We raise cattle and timber. We are right now in the middle of the spring calving season, during which we will have about twenty calves. We should be used to it, nonchalant about it, by now. But every new calf is a thrill, an excitement. To see it emerge, find its legs, and find the milk—what a miracle! Every element of it is a miracle, and awe-inspiring.

To me, it seems like over-simplification to suggest that there is somebody who is overseeing every step of this process. It happens by itself, following the patterns that have developed naturally over countless millennia. And it is a neutral process, neither good nor evil. Every once in a while we get a deformed calf, or a dead calf. We don't presume to blame that on "God," which we would have to do—logically—if we thought God was overseeing the production of new life. And we feel no need to pray to some unseen power to prevent those disappointments. They just happen.

When I wander in the woods, in the silence broken only by the sounds of the birds and the breezes in the treetops, I find great peace in looking at a wildflower or a tree and realizing that the difference between them and me is so minimal. The purpose of the flower is to be, to grow, to reproduce if possible. Or perhaps it really has no purpose. Nobody cares about it, but it doesn't seem to mind. There's nothing wrong with that, for the flower, or for me.

Can an atheist pray? Why not? I don't believe in God—at least not the God as described by the majority of theists—but I DO believe that there is plenty of evidence that we human beings can summon up powers to help us in difficult times. I don't venture to guess whether these powers are within us or outside us, but I don't think it matters what their source is—they are there. And we can benefit from them.

Those who believe in God summon up these powers by calling upon God in prayer. Those who do not believe in God use other methods—meditation, visualization, altered states of consciousness, whatever. They work for the believer, and because they sometimes work, the believer's faith is strengthened, because the prayers are answered. They work just as well for the non-believer.

One doesn't have to give up one's access to these powers just because one has given up belief in God. They are still there. I use them, all the time. Whereas I used to address a prayer: "Dear God, please..." I now simply place myself in a meditative state, relax and put my feelings into words (sometimes only mentally) addressed to whoever or whatever may be listening. Even if it is only some part of my inner self, something happens to bring me peace, self-assurance, confidence. My fears are calmed, my sorrows are soothed, and I am reminded of my unassailable right to my tiny place in the universe, and that somehow everything will turn out all right in the end—or if it doesn't, it won't really matter.

At one time I was participating in a Twelve-Step program, and at the end of each meeting, the group would join hands and recite the "Lord's Prayer." It always bothered me to be addressing "Our Father" when I did not believe in such a being. And yet I did not want to remain silent. So I wrote my own prayer, and no one noticed that the words I was reciting were slightly different from what the others were saying:

richard packham

Atheist Prayer

Our Powers are within,
Whatever be their name.
What they have done, what still may come,
This Earth can yet be as Heaven.
Live then this day, and without dread,
And forgive your own trespasses
As you forgive those who trespass against you.
And be not led into temptation,
But flee away from evil,
For Time is the Healer,
With power to restore me,
Forever and ever, Amen.

My prayer is a snowflake blown by the wind.
My prayer is a flower buzzed by the bees.
My prayer is a bear eating raspberries.
My prayer is an oak tree struck by lightning.

My prayer rolls in on a wave.
My prayer bursts forth as lava.
My prayer burns in the heart.
My prayer is a wordless song.

My prayer is an old woman knitting.
My prayer is a child swinging high.
My prayer is a martial art.
My prayer is performance art.

My prayer sinks into the Earth.
My prayer walks in Beauty.
My prayer is Many.
My prayer is One.

My prayer is for Peace.
My prayer is for an end to suffering.
My prayer leaps like a salmon.
My prayer sits zazen.

My prayer is quilted.
My prayer is piebald.
My prayer is albino.
My prayer is ebony.
My prayer is turquoise.
My prayer is diamond.

susun weed

My prayer is a mantra.
My prayer is a sutra.
My prayer is a Mass in Latin.
My prayer is sung from a tower.

My prayer echoes the holiest sound.
My prayer dances the world into being.
My prayer goes on walk-about.
My prayer is a vision quest gift.

My prayer came to me at dawn.
My prayer will not speak to me.
My prayer is the starry sky.
My prayer is a dewdrop.

My prayer is bound
My prayer is in freedom.
My prayer laughs at itself.
My prayer accepts chaos.

My prayer is in praise.
My prayer is in gratitude.
My prayer is in bliss.
My prayer is in pain.

My prayer is in my breath.
My prayer is in my pocket.
My prayer is in your hands.
My prayer is the smoke spiraling.

Goddesses, Grandmothers, Spirit Sisters, Ancient Ones,
May it be pleasing to you.

Blessed be.
Om Shanti.
Hare Krishna.
Sat Nam.
Hail Mary.
For All My Relations.

As I awaken each morning I am surprised and happy because I am still here after 92 years. I talk to God, or sometimes to Mother Nature, or to Creator of All Things. It's all the same to me, but mostly to God because way back then it was only God. I give thanks for another day on this beautiful and mysterious planet.

My first prayer is for my children and grandson. Thank you God for their very good health and may they always have love, compassion and laughter.

Throughout the day I give thanks for many, many things as they happen.

I ask for help as I hear a crying, hurting dog. As I hear and see threats of an oncoming storm. As I hear of a sick neighbor, and as I drive by a curled-up man lying in the street.

My day is filled with prayers.

Each night I sit on my bed and give thanks for the past day. I ask for these people-killing wars to end and for the military to return home to loved ones, and I pray they can live a good healthy life regardless of the horrible memories of war. And please, God, may we not have future wars.

I pray at this time especially, may our politicians be more worthy of the titles and positions they hold.

I feel each contributor to this book is a link in the chain of world love—a chain with no end.

Many thanks, and always, my unconditional love.

Prayer For The World

Dear God,
We pray for this our world.
We ask that you remove the walls that separate
us and the chains that hold us down.
Use us to create a new world on Earth, one that
reflects Your will, Your vision, Your peace.
In this moment, we recognize the power You
have given us to create anew the world we want.
Today's world, dear Lord, but reflects our past confusion.
Now, in this moment, we ask for new light.
Illumine our minds.
Use us, dear Lord, as never before, as part of a
great and mighty plan for the healing of this world.
May we no longer be at war with each other.
May we no longer be at war with ourselves.
Let us forgive this century and every other, the
evils of history, the pain of our common fears.
Remove from our hearts the illusion that we are separate.
May every nation and every people and every
color and every religion find at last the one
heartbeat we share,
Through You, our common Father/Mother and
the redeemer of our broken dreams.
May we not hold on to yesterday.
May we not obscure Your vision of tomorrow
but rather may You flood our hearts.
Flow through us, work through us, that in our
lives we might see the illumined world.
Create, sustain that world on Earth, dear God,
for us and for our children.

Hallelujah, at the thought,
Praise God, the possibility that such a thing
could come to be, through You, through
Your light that shines within us.
So may it be.
So may it be.
We thank You, Lord.
Amen.

Ma hoe nese. May we be grateful for human intelligence, and may it be free from mental poisons. In all of your magnificence, I ask help for me to understand your presence in all living beings, especially the daily poverty and the suffering human beings. I can see greatness in your love and compassion in the humanitarian work, and it is divine, perfectly pure. Help me to transform my house into a Sacred School for youth; the holy medicine teachers are waiting. Once the youth obtain sacred practice, it will bring the mental calmness to allow the miraculous powers to transform the beauty-way of living your divine life. They will pick up original instructions from the medicine wheel. For it's time—our human intelligence is hungry for this wisdom of rituals practice and for the promise that you answer mothers' prayers.

I pray on my knees ... every single time I receive a baby into the world. I pray in the process: each prenatal checkup, each time I hug an expectant mother, is a prayer. I pray silently when the mother spills her heart to me. I pray often, and with so many results, it is astonishing.

Every morning I say, "Thank YOU," and I call a meeting with my committee of Angels. I assign them jobs:

Dear Angel ... Look after the young single mother in labor.

Angel of strength ... PLEASE comfort the young father who just found out he is HIV positive.

Angels ... One of you go to his wife, and make sure she does not get infected.

Safety Angel ... Please make sure my son wears his helmet on the motorbike.

Angel of money ... Make sure we can pay the bills for the clinic.

Hand-washing Angels, Tooth-brushing Angels, Street-crossing Angels ... Look after my grandchildren.

Milk Angels ... Help the mothers to breastfeed their babies.

Angels of Midwives ... Look after the birth-keepers.

Angels of Peace ... Please don't give up!

Infant CPR

I have shaved God's head and forged
the hum of bees,
to breath life into a flaccid born baby,
to trade a few years of my own time,
a bargain if this one gasps and lives.

She will grow now and dance in a Hindu temple,
and make a shape against
the Balinese sky.

—Robin Lim, from The Geometry of Splitting Souls

You have a great angel with you and her name is Prayer. She is a celestial being of pure light and pure love. Call to her and she will carry the prayers of your heart directly to God. Then mercy, God's benevolence, will reign upon you, and you will be healed. This angelic presence of Prayer lives in every single life particle that exists, for it is life's essence itself. Every cell of every living thing is in prayer—otherwise it would not exist. All you have to do is see this. Every tree, every rock, every molecule of water and of air, all natural things, every cell within them, embodies prayer. Attune to this and you will know the true meaning of prayer. Prayer will bless you.

Prayer is our natural state. In prayer, the Soul is in resting position—in repose. To be in prayer for the Soul is effortless—there is no trying, there is nothing to obtain, and there is nothing to gain. Allow yourself to gently receive the angelic understanding of prayer and Prayer will make herself known to you. Prayer is exquisite. Prayer is holy. Prayer is brilliant. In prayer, there is no separation.

Prayer is where we must live to find the unity among us. Prayer means to simply allow the ego mind to take a breath and move aside. Trust. It's that easy. Listen to the frequency within yourself of your prayer, allow your heart to breathe, allow your heart to open, allow your heart to loosen all constriction, allow your heart to just let go of the human experience and live in your heart's true essence, the experience of "Oneness"—prayer.

Every day, melt into Prayer. Merge your heart into her radiant song. Learn the melody she imbues and then become the master composer of her. Be in the innocence of your prayer. Keep faith. Pray from the deepest, most hidden, private, secret place of your being. Great relief, a sigh, revelation as Prayer calms and rocks and holds you in her arms. Peace. Prayer in her gratitude brings the glories of miraculous salvation.

I pray two ways. Both ways come mostly from the primacy of consciousness and quantum physics. In quantum physics, there is a greater role for intention, but it is often misunderstood. To pray, I first intend. That is the first of four stages. Second, I dedicate my intention for the greater good. The third stage is very crucial because the intention is substantial only if it resonates with the intention of the One, the nonlocal consciousness. I say, "Let the intention come true if it resonates with the intention of nonlocal consciousness." At the fourth stage, as in all spiritual traditions, the prayer ends in silence.

There's another way that I pray. Ultimately, it's the lifestyle that you're looking for: a prayerful lifestyle. Quantum physics gives us a very good theory for the chakras—the places where we feel our feelings viscerally. For example, the heart chakra is where we feel love. I meditate on love and feel the energy at the heart chakra, intensely for a few minutes, and then periodically just to check on whether the energy is still there. If the energy is not there, I bring it back by thinking of people I love and recent memories of feeling love. Then I go on doing my chores. All of the stuff of the world that comes to me during the day keeps me busy, but every once in a while I remember to pray. That is how to make it a habit. What is amazing is that, in the process, you make the heart energy part of your unconscious processing.

This unconscious processing is a new quantum physics discovery. When we are not conscious, we are still processing in the unconscious. Materialist science denies this, but in quantum physics, there are two levels of reality: the transcendent level, which we have access to when we are unconscious; and the conscious manifestation, which is the result of conscious choice. We choose from quantum possibilities the actual events of the manifest experience. We can live in both realities: one when we are not choosing, not collapsing, and the other when we choose and collapse the manifest universe.

We are in a fantastic position if we can guide what we process when we are unconscious. Without any guidance, most people process only what they process when they are conscious, so nothing creative can happen. But by giving your occasional attention to the heart chakra, you guarantee that your heart is open while you process unconsciously. And that is extremely conducive to a creative exploration of love, conflict resolution, and all that.

steve bhaerman

What science is discovering is that prayer works even when religion doesn't.

If anyone asks me how I pray, my simple answer is that I pray the Jesus prayer. It consists simply in repeating the words: "Lord Jesus Christ, Son of God, have mercy on me, a sinner." I have used this prayer now for over forty years and it has become so familiar that it simply repeats itself. Whenever I am not otherwise occupied or thinking of something else, the prayer goes quietly on. Sometimes it is almost mechanical, just quietly repeating itself, and other times it gathers strength and can become extremely powerful.

I give it my own interpretation. When I say, "Lord Jesus Christ, Son of God," I think of Jesus as the Word of God, embracing Heaven and Earth and revealing himself in different ways and under different names and forms to all humanity. I consider that this Word "enlightens everyone coming into the world," and though they may not recognize it, it is present to every human being in the depths of their soul. Beyond word and thought, beyond all signs and symbols, this Word is being secretly spoken in every heart, in every place and at every time. People may be utterly ignorant of it or may choose to ignore it, but whenever or wherever anyone responds to truth or love or kindness, to the demand for justice, concern for others, and care of those in need, they are responding to the voice of the Word. So also when anyone seeks truth or beauty in science, philosophy, poetry or art, they are responding to the invitation of the Word.

I believe that Word took flesh in Jesus of Nazareth, and in him we can find a personal form of the Word to whom we can pray and to whom we can relate in terms of love and intimacy, but I think that he makes himself known to others under different names and forms. What counts is not so much the name and the form as the response in the heart to the hidden mystery, which is present to each one of us in one way or another and awaits our response in faith and love and hope.

When I say, "Have mercy on me, a sinner," I unite myself with all human beings from the beginning of the world, who have experienced separation from God, or from the eternal truth. I realize that, as human beings, we are all separated from God, from the source of our being. We are wandering in a world of shadows, mistaking the outward appearance of people and things for reality. But at all times, something is pressing us to reach beyond the shadows, to face the reality, the truth, the inner meaning of our lives, and so to find God, or whatever name we give to the mystery which enfolds us.

So I say the Jesus prayer, asking to be set free from the illusions of the world, from the innumerable vanities and deceits with which I am surrounded. And I find in the name of Jesus the name that opens my heart and mind to reality. I believe that each one of us has an inner light, an inner guide, which will lead us through the shadows and illusions by which we are surrounded and open our minds to the truth. It may come through poetry or art, or philosophy or science, or more commonly through encounters with people and events, day by day. Personally, I find that meditation, morning and evening, every day, is the best and most direct method of getting in touch with reality. In meditation I try to let go of everything of the outer world of the senses, of the inner world of thoughts, and listen to the inner voice, the voice of the Word, which comes in the silence, in the stillness when all activity of mind and body ceases. Then, in the silence, I become aware of the presence of God, and I try to keep that awareness during the day. On a bus or a train or traveling by air, in work or study or talking and relating to others, I try to be aware of this presence in everyone and in everything. And the Jesus prayer is what keeps me aware of the presence.

So prayer for me is the practice of the presence of God in all situations, in the midst of noise and distractions of all sorts—of pain and suffering and death—and in times of peace and quiet, of joy and friendship, of prayer and silence, the presence is always there. For me, the Jesus prayer is just a way of keeping in the presence of God.

How do I pray? How beautiful. It's such an important thing to do. I think many people are frightened of prayer and don't do it nearly enough. There should be an undercurrent of prayer in everything, because everything is potentially a prayer—every reaction, every gesture, every movement, every inner thought.

Everything is praying. One of the most amazing things that happens as you begin to awaken is that you truly understand that everything is, in its own way, praying to God and praising God. Birds are praying and praising when they sing; stones are praying and praising by being stones; someone is praying and praising, laughing in the light; the gazelle is praying and praising, leaping; the lion is praying and praising, running through the couch grass. The entire universe is a constant song of prayer and praise.

There's nothing else really going on. And the problem of human beings is that they have invented all kinds of ways of denying this and destroying this sacred fabric, which is why it's so endangered right now. All of the truly enlightened people I've met—and there have been about three of them, of course—have been people who were in constant prayer.

Anything I would have to say about prayer would really have to involve talking about two of my greatest teachers, who really showed me the centrality of prayer to any kind of awakened life. The first was the great Mahāyāna Buddhist teacher, Thuksey Rinpoche, who I met in Ladakh. I had the honor of being with him as he began to go through his dying process. I wasn't there when he died, but I was there when he was tremendously sick. I had a fantasy that, since he was so awake, he wouldn't need to do anything or meditate or pray— he would just be in the simple state and all would unfold. But that was my fantasy, and he showed me by his constant prayer, by the way in which he constantly prayed so beautifully and so sincerely that, for him, prayer was the finest and highest way to stay in constant communion with the Great Emptiness, the Great Nothing, the

Great Everything. Those who were with him when he was dying told me that he was praying up to the very end.

The second person who really showed me the truth of what St. Paul means when he says, "Pray constantly, pray incessantly," which is the universal advice of all the great mystics, was Rumi. He quotes the verse from the Koran, "They are constantly at their prayers." And Rumi says that the person who is truly in love with the beloved doesn't just confine their prayers to set times or set pieces or set occasions, but makes of every moment a prayer that they offer to the beloved, which means really perfuming your every thought and action as much as you can with love and praise and celebration and compassion.

I prepare for prayer by bringing my awareness into my heart chakra, where I imagine a golden flame, representing my divine essence, burning warmly.

While feeling the golden flame, I contemplate gratitude for the infinite opportunities that this precious human life and earthen body offer for growth, healing and evolution.

I pause and allow myself to feel gratitude awakening so strongly that the heart flame grows warmer and brighter, transmuting and purifying any negative energy in my field.

I pause to acknowledge and honor the Heart Essence—which is the enlightened essence of all the Masters, Buddhas, Bodhisattvas, Deities and the Higher Self—that lives within me.

From this centered, expanded place, I ground my light into the Earth below as an offering of gratitude for our dear Mother. Once connected, I feel Mother Earth's blessings arise from her depths, upward into my root chakra, travelling up through the center of my body and out the crown of my head, connecting with the chakras above me. Then the blessings of above and below merge and rain down into my crown and into the golden flame burning in my heart.

Once the Heart Essence is ignited in my awareness, I follow the golden flame deep into the Sacred Inner Temple in my heart to the candle I see burning on the altar there.

I merge with my Inner Self, the part of my being that resides there, and I tune into the Prayerfield of the Heart Essence, feeling the forces of love, light and healing move me to prayer.

"Om bhur bhuvah svah
tat savitur varenyam
bhargo devasya dhimahi
dhiyo yo nah prochodayat."

Throughout all realms of experience
"That"
essential nature illuminating existence
is the adorable
One.
May all beings perceive through
subtle and meditative intellect
the magnificent brilliance
of enlightened awareness.

Gayatri Mantra

"We meditate on the glory of that Being who has produced this
universe; may He enlighten our minds."

Swami Vivekananda
1915 Translation

From a very young age, I have prayed with the Gayatri mantra. In my tradition, starting to recite the Gayatri mantra is done in an initiation, similar to the Bat Mitzvah and the Bar Mitzvah of the Jewish tradition. When I was eleven, my dad arranged a Thread Ceremony. During the ceremony, I was taught how to recite the Gayatri mantra. It is a four-line mantra, and it is also a prayer. It is probably one of the oldest, and is considered to be one of the most powerful mantras. There are many interpretations of the meaning and benefit of the Gayatri mantra—people say it will bring you light and intelligence, and that it will make your wishes come true. They also say you will always be truthful if you recite this mantra.

Saying the mantra with the right intention sends me into a deep, meditative, reflective place.

My initiation into the power of prayer was through the Gayatri mantra. This prayer for the awakening of all sentient beings has a very special place in my heart. Through this ancient chant, I discovered that the love I had for all my life been seeking outside myself was right here inside my own heart. Without exaggeration, it is the greatest gift I can possibly imagine. To sing this prayer opens me again and again to feeling the "big me," to allowing the soothing nectar of compassion to pour from my heart. This prayer is the unwavering promise that no one has to suffer alone or be forgotten.

Prayer is a language that can express the very depths of the heart, even if the form of prayer taught to us in church or synagogue no longer feels very natural.

Prayer doesn't have to happen on our knees with our hands folded. Simply being present with this moment is prayer.

Prayer can be dancing, it can be singing, it can be opening our arms wide on a hilltop, screaming at the top of our lungs. It can be closing our eyes, floating in the ocean, listening to the pulse of life.

Prayer can be taking a walk without thinking, opening ourselves to the trees, the leaves, and the smell of the soil. It can be walking, as if we are kissing the face of the Earth with our feet. Prayer can be listening.

Prayer can be a ritual; it can be lighting a candle and incense or chanting sacred words and sounds. It can be remembering and contemplating the wisdom of the ancestors or laughing for thirty minutes a day from deep down in our bellies.

Prayer is simply a way of opening our hearts; it is a way of expressing gratitude and surrendering to life in all its dimensions.

I surrender and glimpse, if only for a moment, the assumption of a separate self, and in that instant I am merged into the totality of existence.

After I am up and dressed, I sit in a comfortable chair and enter what I call my "quiet time." Reminding myself of the Apostle John's assurance that, "Now we are the sons of God, and it doth not appear what we shall be; but we know that when He shall appear, we shall be like Him, for we shall see him as he is" (1 John 3:2), I continue my way through the New Testament by reading a passage from the Bible. (This morning it was from the Book of Acts.)

Then I pray: first for the members of my nuclear family, naming them by name and praying that they will have rewarding, fulfilling days.

Finally I pray for myself, for as a familiar spiritual has it: "Not my brother nor my sister but it's me, oh Lord; standing in the need of prayer."

I begin with gratitude for my health and for being a part of a loving family. From there, I pray for wisdom in the way I maneuver the events of the day.

That is followed by intercessory prayer: praying for friends or associates whom I happen to know are in trouble of one sort or another—illness, whatever.

I close my "quiet time" by emptying my mind of thoughts and meditating wordlessly for perhaps fifteen minutes. Then I'm ready for my coffee.

"Help, I prayed, help. (Help, help is one of the best prayers I know; you just have to be prepared for some bizarre responses.)"
—Maeve, the Celtic Magdalen from *Bright Dark Madonna*

Also in my prayer vocabulary: please, thank you, I love you, and moments beyond words (always a gift of grace for someone who is verbose). Help, help! has predominated this year, the year of hospital. After a two-month bout with brain cancer, a close friend of mine died. Following her memorial service, my sister had major surgery with major complications. (She is all right now. Thank you!) As of this writing, my husband is (thank you!) about to come home after being hospitalized with babesiosis, a tick-borne disease similar to malaria. We are also in the midst of selling a legally-complicated property and preparing to move. (Help, help!)

The other day I managed to quiet myself enough to check my soul-mail. My late friend showed up with a message: *Empty your prayer basket.* The prayer basket, made of alder wands and copper wire, is something my friend, a brilliant artist, helped me construct. It sits on my altar, and when people (including me) request prayers, I write their names and a few words on a piece of paper and drop it in the basket. Over the last few months it has gotten very full and started to look more like a wastebasket than a prayer basket. *Empty it,* my friend said, *and don't fill it again.*

That night I went outside just before a thunderstorm and burned the prayers with a prayer that the all the prayers be answered in whatever way, bizarre and beautiful, the great mystery devises. The prayer basket is back on my altar. I contemplate its bare-branched, bare-boned beauty, empty and full of all the things I can't fix or fathom.

father william hart mcnichols

Dear Abba, Father,
Thank you for hearing me.
I know you always hear me.
Keep me faithful, and more than that, full of
Spirit, Zeal, Love and Life in the vocations you have given to me,
as your Priest called upon to heal by offering the Eucharist and
    bringing
the Gospel of Glad Tidings of Great Joy to all nations, all
    people, but
especially the destitute of heart and circumstance, and of
    course, your beloved outcasts.
Most of all in this Way, let me See people, as your Son sees
    them. His gaze
is transforming as he sees into the heart and soul and erodes
    our faults,
especially mine...as he never gives up on our transformation
    into him.
Let me see people so that they know they have been seen and
    loved, even at a
distance. And forgive me for those I cannot see and thus hurt or
    wound by
my inability to love them.
Father, don't let me get too down or paralyzed by my own or others
    suffering, but allow me to have faith and trust in you that you
    are God and can do
all things and I am just your worker.
I would like to be like the saints who can heal with a touch or
glance...heal everyone of everything, but this is only possible
    through your
grace, and at moments you use your servants this way...and at
    others, we

204

stumble along.

And now the icons, images and "painted arrows." Let me hit the center of

the heart and soul with each work of my hand. And one day, if it be your

will, place them in the Great Treasury of Grace in Holy Church, the Bride of

your Son.

From my union and petitions to you, these images flow, they are your gifts

to me and to anyone who also receives them. I know well I could never do

even one without the movement of the Indwelling Spirit who guides even the

most primitive strokes of pencil and brush.

As people are hungry for truth, hope and love, let these works fill them with

spiritual nourishment. Let the images come to life for them to guide them

and return the love they feel while gazing, while contemplating.

And Dear Lord, let me do as many more as you want, shooting my painted

arrows into suffering hearts and souls...giving them the Hope and Joy which

signal the light of your presence.

Thank you, Father, for hearing me; I know you always hear me.

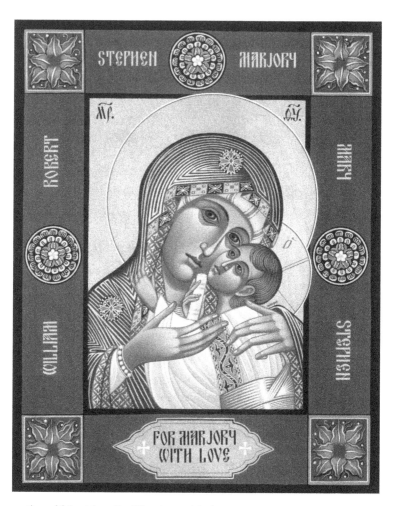

mother of fairest love © william h. mcnichols

contributors

sharif abdullah

Sharif Abdullah, JD, is an author and advocate for inclusivity and the social/ spiritual transformation of society. Sharif is a transformationist, working to align our global human societies with our common spiritual values. His vision and work for a world that works for all beings stems from his spiritual awareness and his experiences in over a hundred distinct cultures in over forty countries. Sharif is founder and director of Commonway Institute. His books include *The Power of One: Authentic Leadership in Turbulent Times,* the award-winning *Creating a World That Works for All* and *Seven Seeds for a New Society*. Sharif is a graduate-level adjunct professor of conflict resolution at Portland State University, a senior advisor to Sarvodaya in Sri Lanka and is the recipient of numerous awards and recognitions.

www.commonway.org

patch adams

Patch Adams is best known for his work as a medical doctor and a clown and as a social activist who has devoted forty-two years to changing America's health care system. He believes that laughter, joy and creativity are an integral part of the healing process. The Gesundheit Institute is a project in holistic medical care based on the belief that one cannot separate the health of the individual from the health of the family, the community, the world and the health care system itself. Patch created a hospital—free for all people—that will be fully modern at 10 percent of the cost. The cleaning person and the surgeon will make the same salary—$300/ month—and all permanent staff will live there as a communal village, eliminating 85 percent of the environmental footprint. www.patchadams.org

sri mata amritanandamayi devi

Spiritual leader, humanitarian and visionary Sri Mata Amritananda-mayi Devi, known throughout the world simply as "Amma," has served the world-community for decades, imparting wisdom, strength and inspiration. Through her extraordinary acts of love, inner strength and self-sacrifice, Amma has endeared herself to millions and inspired thousands to follow in her path of selfless service.

Receiving Amma's embrace, many feel inspired to offer selfless service to those in need. In this way, this simple yet powerful act as a mother's embrace—has become both catalyst and symbol for the growing international network of humanitarian initiatives known as "Embracing the World."®
www.embracingtheworld.org

arjuna ardagh

Arjuna Ardagh is an Awakening Coach, writer and public speaker. He has trained more than 1,300 people to become facilitators of Awakening. He is the author of seven books, including the 2005 No. 1 national bestseller *The Translucent Revolution*, featured in *O*, the Oprah Winfrey magazine. His latest book, *Better than Sex*, is the complete introduction to Awakening Coaching. He has been a speaker at conferences all over the world and has appeared on TV, radio and in print media in twelve countries. He is a member of the Transformational Leadership Council. He lives with his wife, Chameli Ardagh, and their two teenage sons in California.
www.arjunaardagh.com.

chameli ardagh

Chameli Ardagh is a passionate practitioner of embodied feminine spirituality and the founder of the Awakening Women Institute.

She is the initiator of an international network of Women's Temple Groups and the author of two books on feminine spirituality and embodiment.

www.awakeningwomen.com

kenny ausubel

Kenny Ausubel is an award-winning social entrepreneur, author, journalist and filmmaker. His work has long been at the forefront of the environmental, health and progressive social-change movements. He is the CEO and cofounder of Bioneers, an educational nonprofit that highlights breakthrough solutions for restoring people and planet, and co-founded the biodiversity organic company Seeds of Change. His film *Hoxsey: When Healing Becomes a Crime* (which won a "Best Censored Stories" journalism award) played in theaters, on HBO and international TV and at a special screening for members of Congress which was featured on National Public Radio. Kenny has written and edited several books, including *Dreaming the Future: Reimagining Civilization in the Age of Nature*.

www.bioneers.org

carolyn baker

Carolyn Baker, Ph.D., is the author of *Collapsing Consciously: Transformative Truths For Turbulent Times, Sacred Demise: Walking The Spiritual Path Of Industrial Civilization's Collapse* and *Navigating The Coming Chaos: A Handbook For Inner Transition*. She lives in Boulder, Colo., where she works with Transition Colorado. A former psychotherapist, she offers life coaching for people who want to live more resiliently in the present as they prepare for the future.

www.carolynbaker.net

margaret behan

Red Spider Woman—"Ba nee uth sai"—is Margaret Behan's Arapahoe name; her Cheyenne name is "Ma'ee Vehoe ga'ee." Her mother's people are Southern Cheyenne, who are keepers of the Sacred Arrows. Her father's people are Northern Cheyenne and they are keepers of the Sacred Medicine Hat. Her father's mother was Arapahoe, the keepers of the Sacred Pipe Watonga. Margaret spent her childhood in Oklahoma, and went on to mission and government boarding schools. Her career has been making storyteller dolls out of natural clay that represent figures from stories and legends and expresses their great love for each other and their people.

robyn benson

For twenty-one years, Dr. Robyn Benson, DOM, has been the mother of two and an adventure enthusiast, world traveler, speaker and author who loves to help and inspire each and every patient to achieve optimal, radiant and sustainable health. In addition to building Santa Fe Soul, a twenty-first-century health care center that is the home of twenty-five practitioners and has a vision that is locally focused and globally expressed, Robyn is now onto what she calls her legacy: the creation of a movement to change the face of health care, the Self-Care Revolution. www.santafesoul.com
www.jointheselfcarerevolution.com

steve bhaerman

Steve Bhaerman is an internationally known author, humorist and workshop leader. For more than twenty-five years, he has written and performed as Swami Beyondananda, the "Cosmic Comic." Swami's comedy has been described both as "comedy disguised as wisdom" and "wisdom disguised as comedy." Noted author

Marianne Williamson has called him "the Mark Twain of our generation." Since 2005, Steve has written a political blog with a spiritual perspective, "Notes From the Trail." His latest book, written with cellular biologist Bruce H. Lipton, Ph.D., is *Spontaneous Evolution: Our Positive Future and a Way to Get There From Here.* www.wakeuplaughing.com

tessa bielecki

Tessa Bielecki was a Carmelite monk for almost forty years, co-founded the Spiritual Life Institute and served as Mother Abbess of the contemplative community until 2005. She teaches at Colorado College, gives lectures and retreats, participates in East-West dialogues and writes. She is the author of three books on St. Teresa of Avila, and recently recorded *Teresa of Avila: The Book of My Life* for Shambhala Audio and *Wild at Heart: Radical Teachings of the Christian Mystics* for Sounds True. Her great passion is the desert. She lives alone in a log cabin in Crestone, Colo., in the spirit of the ancient Fathers and Mothers of the Desert, and co-founded the Desert Foundation with Father Dave Denny in 2005. www.desertfound.org

venerable bhikkhu bodhi

Venerable Bhikkhu Bodhi is a Theravada Buddhist monk from New York City. He was ordained in Sri Lanka in 1972 and lived in Asia for twenty-four years. For eighteen years he was editor for the Buddhist Publication Society in Kandy. Ven. Bodhi has many important publications to his credit, the most recent being a full translation of the Anguttara Nikaya, *Numerical Discourses of the Buddha*. In 2008, he founded Buddhist Global Relief, a nonprofit providing hunger relief and education in countries suffering from chronic poverty and malnutrition. He is president of the Buddhist Association of the

United States and lives at Chuang Yen Monastery in Carmel, N.Y.
www.buddhistglobalrelief.org

george boeree

George Boeree is a retired psychology professor at Shippensburg
University, Pa., where he taught personality theories and the history
of psychology, among other topics. Born in the Netherlands, he
grew up on Long Island, N.Y. He is married to Judith Kovarik and
has three grown daughters and two grandchildren.
www.webspace.ship.edu/cgboer
www.boeree.socialpsychology.org

gregg braden

New York Times bestselling author Gregg Braden is internationally
renowned as a pioneer in bridging science and spirituality. Following
a successful career as a computer geologist for *Phillips Petroleum*
during the 1970s energy crisis, he worked as a senior computer
systems designer with *Martin Marietta Defense Systems* during the
last years of the Cold War. In 1991 he became the first technical
operations manager for *Cisco Systems,* where he led the development
of the global support team that insures the reliability of today's
internet. For more than 25 years, Gregg has searched high mountain
villages, remote monasteries and forgotten texts to uncover their
timeless secrets. His work is now featured on the History Channel,
the Discovery Channel, the Sci Fi Channel, ABC and NBC. To date,
Gregg's discoveries have led to such paradigm-shattering books
as: *The Isaiah Effect, The God Code, The Divine Matrix* and *Fractal Time.*
His latest book is *Deep Truth: Igniting the Origin of Our Origin, History,
Destiny and Fate.* Gregg's work is published in 17 languages and 33
countries and shows us beyond any reasonable doubt that the key to

our future lies in the wisdom of our past.
www.greggbraden.com

rev. cynthia brix

Rev. Cynthia Brix is a contemplative interfaith minister and co-director of Satyana Institute. She is cofounder of the Gender Reconciliation International project, which conducts training programs for reconciliation between women and men in South Africa, Australia, India, Colombia and North America. Cynthia is co-author of *Women Healing Women* and a contributing author of *Divine Duality: The Power of Reconciliation Between Women and Men*. Cynthia organized an international conference in Italy that brought women spiritual leaders together and produced a DVD from this conference titled *Cultivating Women's Spiritual Mastery*.
www.satyana.org
www.GRworld.org

jeff brown

A former criminal lawyer and psychotherapist, Jeff Brown is the author of *Soulshaping: A Journey of Self-Creation* and *Ascending with Both Feet on the Ground*. He is also the author of the viral blog *Apologies to the Divine Feminine* and the producer and key journeyer in the award-winning spiritual documentary *Karmageddon,* which also stars Ram Dass, Seane Corn, Wah!, David Life, Deva Premal and Miten. Jeff's newest book, *Love It Forward*, endorsed by bestselling authors Andrew Harvey and Caroline Myss, is another book of impactful quotes and writings, with a strong emphasis on love and relationship.
www.soulshaping.com

adam bucko

Adam Bucko is a co-author of *Occupy Spirituality: A Radical Vision for a New Generation*. An activist and spiritual director to many of New York's homeless youth, he is a cofounder of the Reciprocity Foundation, empowering homeless youth to break the cycle of poverty and HAB, a contemplative fellowship focused on training young people in radical spirituality and sacred activism. He collaborates with spiritual leaders across religious traditions and mentors young people, helping them discover a spiritual life in the twenty-first century and how to live deeply from the heart in service of compassion and justice. Adam is a recipient of several awards, and his work has appeared on ABC News, CBS and NBC, and in the *New York Daily News* and the *National Catholic Reporter* as well as *Ode*, *Yoga International* and *Sojourner* magazines.
www.reciprocityfoundation.org
www.adambucko.com

sita jamieson caddle

Sita has been chanting in the United States for the past 25 years and has led chanting evenings in Singapore, Bali and India. She started within the Hindu tradition of Kirtan and expanded out to all traditions to reach broader audiences. She blends sacred poetry into her evenings, weaving a tapestry of chant and spoken word that is powerful and celebratory. Sita is a teacher in the art of chanting and her classes allow people to become more fluid in their own ability to sing. She also works with sound as a healing modality combined with energy work to create a complete healing session. A native of Ireland, Sita feels her voice comes out of her Celtic roots; its full resonance expresses an ancient, earthy form of song. She is a disciple of Neem Karoli Baba and has performed with Krishna Das, Ram Dass and Baghavan Das.
www.sitachants.com

mariana caplan

Mariana Caplan, Ph.D., MFT, is a psychotherapist, yogi and the author of six books in the fields of psychology and spirituality, including the award-winning *Eyes Wide Open: Cultivating Discernment on the Spiritual Path*, the seminal *Halfway Up the Mountain: The Error of Premature Claims to Enlightenment* and *The Guru Question: The Perils and Rewards of Choosing a Spiritual Teacher*. As a psychotherapist, she specializes in using somatic approaches to therapy to support spiritual practitioners and teachers of all traditions and religions to heal trauma and thrive, as well as working with complex spiritual traumas within spiritual communities. As a yogi, she founded and teaches the Yoga & Psyche Method, which integrates the insights of somatic psychology, trauma research, neuroscience and yogic practices.

www.realspirituality.com

george cappannelli

George Cappannelli is a writer, sculptor, Emmy-Award-winning producer/director, corporate and political consultant and cofounder of AgeNation, a media and events company dedicated to informing, inspiring and engaging people in critical challenges and opportunities of the second half of life. His nonfiction books include *Say Yes To Change, Authenticity, I Dream of A New America, It's About Time* and *Do Not Go Quietly: A Guide To Living Consciously & Aging Wisely For People Who Weren't Born Yesterday*. His consulting clients include some of the country's leading Fortune 500 companies, government agencies, nonprofits and U.S. senators and presidential candidates.

www.georgecappannelli.com

www.agenation.com

www.donotgoquietlythebook.com

sedena cappannelli

Sedena is the co-founder of AgeNation, a digital media company supporting people ages forty and over to live more conscious and engaging lives. She is recognized nationally as a speaker, award-winning author and Enlivened Ageing and wellness consultant. In her talks and programs, Sedena combines personal development, energy management and corporate strategies to help individuals and organizations create greater balance, vitality, productivity and purpose, and includes practical wisdom from her books *Say Yes To Change, Authenticity* and the bestseller *Do Not Go Quietly*. She is also the creator of *P.E.P.—Personal Energy Program*, a groundbreaking personal wellness DVD.
www.agenation.com

daniel craig

Daniel Craig is a Doctor of Oriental Medicine in Santa Fe, N.M., who practices in a community acupuncture clinic. He served in the Regular Army and Army National Guard from 1981 through 1993 and did one tour in Iraq/Kuwait during Operation Desert Storm. Daniel is a member of Veterans For Peace—Joan Duffy Chapter in Santa Fe He has a bachelor's degree in psychology and a master's degree in oriental medicine. He is a native New Mexican.

elizabeth cunningham

Elizabeth Cunningham is best known as the author of *The Maeve Chronicles*, a series of award-winning novels featuring the feisty Celtic Magdalen, who is no one's disciple. Also a counselor in private practice, she recently moved from the east side of New York's Hudson River to the west.
www.elizabethcunninghamwrites.com
www.passionofmarymagdalen.com

chris deckker

Musician, artist and visionary entrepreneur Chris Deckker has been involved in the arts and entertainment industry for over thirty years. His extensive experience spans every level of the industry, from artistic to business. He is the cofounder of one of the United Kingdom's most successful underground electronic music clubs, "Return to the Source" and record label, which gained international recognition in the '90s, and is the founder of the electronic music group Medicine Drum, which was signed to Virgin Records USA. In 1997 he founded "Earthdance International—The Global Festival for Peace," which has grown to become the world's biggest synchronized dance event with over three hundred and fifty locations in sixty-five countries involved each year. Originally aimed at supporting Tibet, Earthdance has been described by the office of his Holiness the Dalai Lama as "the most successful global event of its kind aimed at supporting the Tibetan people." Earthdance now supports global charities worldwide. Chris currently lives in Byron Bay, Australia, and is the co-director of UPLIFT, a hybrid eco-conference and music festival. www.upliftfestival.com

elayne doughty

Elayne Kalila Doughty, MA, MFT, is the founder of Soulful Women, Planet Breathe, the Soul Spa and the Queens of Transformation. She is a psychotherapist, speaker, ordained priestess soul-midwife, priestess empowerment coach and women's empowerment expert. With her extensive background in soul transformation, the divine feminine, recovery, addictions, trauma, mental health, she has over twenty years of experience working with women who are transforming a painful past to a powerful present and an extraordinary future. Elayne is a sought-after teacher and speaker in the fields of women's spirituality, healing, transformation

and leadership.
www.elaynedoughty.com

donna eden

Donna Eden, a pioneer in the field of energy medicine for thirty-five years, is among the field's most sought, joyous and authoritative spokespersons. Able to clairvoyantly "see" the body's energies since childhood, her healing abilities are legendary. Her book *Energy Medicine* has been translated into eighteen languages and was named the Health Book of the Year at the prestigious Nautilus Book Awards. Its sequel, *Energy Medicine for Women*, won gold medals in two national competitions. More than 80,000 people have attended Donna's classes and she has trained more than seven hundred and fifty practitioners who are fully certified in her approach to energy medicine.
www.innersource.net

normandi ellis

Normandi Ellis is a spiritualist medium and the author of ten books of fiction and nonfiction. Her nonfiction is rooted in her studies and travels in Egypt and includes the spiritual classic *Awakening Osiris*. Her most recent books from Bear & Co. are *Invoking the Scribes of Ancient Egypt* and *Imagining the World into Existence*. Her recent fiction, *Going West,* was published by Wind Publications. She facilitates spiritual travel through Egypt in conjunction with Shamanic Journeys.
www.normandiellis.com.

patricia ellsberg

Patricia Ellsberg is a social change activist, meditation teacher and coach. She reaches thousands of people worldwide, leading guided meditations for the *Awakening Joy Course* and teleseminars on *Finding Mother-Love Within* and—together with her sister, Barbara Marx Hubbard—on *The Emergence Process: The Shift from Ego to Essence.* She has been a lifelong partner to Daniel Ellsberg and in their first year of marriage helped him release the top-secret Pentagon Papers, which contributed to ending the Vietnam War. A central theme of her life has been creating a bridge between political activism and spiritual experience.

www.patriciaellsberg.net

dr. masaru emoto

Masaru Emoto was born in Japan in July 1943. In 1986 he established the IHM Corporation in Tokyo. In 1992 he received a certification from the Open International University as a Doctor of Alternative Medicine. He began to discover the mystery of water as he learned the concept of micro-cluster water and magnetic resonance analysis technology. Eventually, he realized that it was in the frozen crystal form that water showed us its true nature through. He has gained worldwide acclaim through his groundbreaking research and discovery that water is deeply connected to our individual and collective consciousness. He is the author of the best-selling books *Message from Water, The Hidden Messages in Water* and *The True Power of Water, The Messages from Water and the Universe* and others. He is a long-time advocate for peace in relation to water. He is currently the president of International Hado Membership and the chairman of the board of the nonprofit organization EMOTO PEACE PROJECT, where he works toward achieving world peace through water. Since the Fukushima nuclear disaster of 3/11 of 2011, he has been helping the people of Fukushima and is giving "angel water" for free, as well as lecturing and providing Hado counseling in the Fukushima area. www.masaru-emoto.net

jennifer esperanza

Jennifer Esperanza is a culture and art photographer based in Santa Fe, N.M. She documented the humanitarian work in South India of Amma and her devotees after the Asian tsunami in 2004 and photographed in New Orleans after Hurricane Katrina. She has photographed some of the greatest social-justice and earth-justice activists of our time, including Van Jones, Dr. Jane Goodall, Bill McKibben, Gloria Steinem and Tim DeChristopher. She also photographs music, fashion, culture, nature and erotica, and makes her own art. Road trips, travel, art and the ocean are some of her passions. Her work is known for its humanity, sensuality and beauty. She prays thanks with every click of her camera shutter. Jennifer's motto is "Drowning in Beauty, Devoted to Love." www.jenniferesperanza.com

patricia flasch

Patricia Flasch has a master's degree in counseling from the University of Wisconsin and was a trainer and marketing director for Cornucopia, a human potential school. Patricia had a large private practice in counseling in Seattle, and then opened LEADING FROM THE HEART in Denver, Colo. Patricia designed and taught seminar topics on "Relationships in Paradise" (Maui) and "The Psychology of Money" (Stockholm, Sweden). Patricia operates today as a soul mentor from Santa Fe, N.M. Her recent book, *Becoming a Love Dog*, is available on Amazon. Her current teaching involves using creativity as a force for conscious aging. She has clients worldwide.
www.patriciaflasch.com

matthew fox

Matthew Fox is the author of thirty-one books on spirituality and culture, which have been translated into fifty-one languages, and is an innovator in birthing new forms of worship (the Cosmic Mass) and education (the Yellawe Institute program for inner city youth and the University of Creation Spirituality, which thrived for twenty-nine years instructing adults in their own mystical and prophetic potential). Matthew is an Episcopal priest (for thirty-four years he was a Dominican priest, but was expelled from the Catholic priesthood by Cardinal Ratzinger), and his books include *Prayer: A Radical Response to Life; Original Blessing, Hildegard of Bingen: A Saint for Our Times; The Hidden Spirituality of Men; A Spirituality Named Compassion* and *A New Reformation.*
www.matthewfox.org

Arun Gandhi worked as a journalist for the *Times of India*, Mumbai, for thirty years before coming to the United States to lecture on Gandhi and his philosophy of nonviolence at universities around the country and Europe. During the course of his life, he has rescued one hundred and twenty-eight abandoned newborn babies and found loving homes for them, and established cooperative programs in Indian villages, that have transformed the lives of over a million people. He is a much sought-after motivational speaker. www.gandhiforchildren.org

Sharon Gannon is the co-creator with David Life of the Jivamukti Yoga Method, a path to enlightenment through compassion for all beings. A student of Shri Brahmananda Sarasvati, Swami Nirmalananda, Sri K. Pattabhi Jois and Shyamdas, she is a pioneer in teaching yoga as spiritual activism and relating ancient teachings to the modern world. Sharon is also a musician and writer. *Sharanam,* is her latest album. Her books include *Jivamukti Yoga, The Art of Yoga, Cats and Dogs Are People Too!,* and *Yoga and Vegetarianism*. She writes a monthly blog for www.jivamuktiyoga.com.

Jeremy Geffen, MD, FACP, is a medical oncologist, a leading expert in integrative medicine and oncology and author of the highly acclaimed book *The Journey Through Cancer: Healing and Transforming the Whole Person*. He has devoted his career to developing the field of whole-person medicine and cancer care and is creator of the pioneering integrative medicine and oncology program, *The Seven Levels of Healing*®. He has more than thirty years of experience exploring the great spiritual and healing traditions of the world. www.geffenvisions.com

michael gelb

Michael J. Gelb is the world's leading authority on the application of genius thinking to personal and organizational development. A pioneer in the fields of creative thinking, accelerated learning and innovative leadership, he has authored fourteen books on creativity and innovation, including the international bestseller, *How to Think Like Leonardo Da Vinci: Seven Steps to Genius Every Day.* His latest book is *Creativity On Demand: How to Ignite and Sustain the Fire of Genius.* www.michaelgelb.com

norma gentile

Norma Gentile, a professional soprano and sound shaman, has combined a performance career with a private practice of energy healing for over twenty years. Her formal training in music (she holds a master's from the University of Michigan) and her studies in subtle energy have helped Norma understand how sound affects our ability to heal. Over the years, Norma developed her own ability as a spiritual channel for those who teach (Archangel Michael), those who heal (Nature) and those who do both (the Hathors). She continues to offer meditation concerts and coach those who want to more fully utilize their own voices and healing abilities. www.healingchants.com

amit goswami

Amit Goswami, Ph.D., is a retired professor of physics from the University of Oregon at Eugene. He is a pioneer of the new paradigm "science within consciousness," an idea he explicated in his seminal book *The Self-Aware Universe*, in which he also solved the quantum measurement problem elucidating the famous observer effect. Amit has written nine other popular books based on his research

in quantum physics and consciousness. He was featured in the film *What the Bleep Do We Know?* and the award-winning documentary of his life and work, *The Quantum Activist*.
www.amitgoswami.org

alex grey

Alex Grey is a visionary artist and leader in the spiritual creative movement. Best known for his paintings, which "X-ray" multiple dimensions of reality, Alex's art interweaves physical and biological anatomy with psychic and spiritual energies. His visual meditation on the nature of life and consciousness, the subject of his art, is contained in three books, *Sacred Mirrors*, *Transfigurations* and *Net of Being*. His philosophy and poetry is shared in his books *The Mission of Art* and *Art Psalms*, which reflects on art as a spiritual practice. His art was featured on the historic album art, video animations and stage design for the cult/metal band Tool. The international entheogen community has embraced Alex Grey as an important mapmaker and spokesperson for visionary realms. Alex and his wife, the artist Allyson Grey, are cofounders of Chapel of Sacred Mirrors (CoSM), an interfaith church and pillar of worldwide Visionary Culture.
www.alexgrey.com
www.cosm.org

allyson grey

Allyson Grey is an artist whose paintings have been exhibited and sold internationally. As the editor and co-author of over a dozen books and journals, Allyson has been a lecturer, educator and muse to artists for over thirty years. The symbol system in her paintings represents an essential worldview comprised of chaos, order and secret writing. For Allyson, chaos symbolizes distinctions and entropy in the physical world. Order, which is composed of

interconnected harmonious patterns, suggests the transcendental unity called heaven or the infinite divine. Secret writing, comprised of 20 unpronounceable letters, represents the spirit of communication irreducible to concepts, windows to inner concepts manifested in the material world. Cofounder of the Chapel of Sacred Mirrors, Allyson is a community leader who holds an MFA from Tufts University. She has been the wife and partner of artist Alex Grey since 1975.
www.allysongrey.com
www.cosm.org

father bede griffiths

Bede Griffiths, born Alan Richard Griffiths, was born in England in 1906. He converted to Catholicism in the early 1930s and soon after joined the Benedictine monastery Prinknash Abbey and took the name Bede. He later served as a Prior of Farnborough and then Pluscardin, during which time he gained an interest in Indian thought. He asked to go to India to set up a monastic foundation, but was denied. Later he was sent to India by the same abbot, but was to serve under the local bishop. From 1955 to1958, he joined Father Francis Mahieu Acharya at Kurisumala Ashram (Mountain of the Cross), where they developed a Syriac rite monastic liturgy. Griffiths took the Sanskrit name Dhayananda, meaning "bliss of prayer." In 1963, he conducted a trip to the United States in which he engaged in an East-West dialogue.

lama gyurme

Master painter and craftsman Lama Gyurme was born in Tanay, Tibet, in 1969. When he was fifteen, his family sent him to the Mindroling monastery upon the invitation of the head monk to study painting and traditional arts. His first teacher was from Kham (Guangzhou), located in Eastern Tibet. After initial study, he went to live with his principal teacher, Lama Tsekyab, in order to fully absorb the rich tradition of Tibetan painting, of which his teacher was a master. The famous paintings of Korkyim Monastery were created by his teacher during the period when Tibetans were once again allowed to worship and rebuild their temples and monasteries. While still young, Gyurme became an adept in Tibetan ritual and monastery traditions. He was the manager and rule keeper of the monastery and led chants at Mindroling until 1998, and painted or assisted in the restoration of hundreds of the temple paintings. In 1998 he was invited to teach painting at the Shanshung Institute in Italy, one of the most important Tibetan Buddhist centers outside of Tibet. He spent the next two years teaching Westerners traditional Tibetan art and sculpture. During his tenure at the Shanshung Institute, he studied Italian and English and wrote an important history of Tibetan art in Tibetan.

www.lamagyurmed.com

www.glasfoundation.org

deirdre hade

Deirdre Hade is a spiritual teacher, master healer, mystic, poet and visionary leader in the ancient arts of the wisdom traditions of light. She is the founder of the Radiance Healing and Radiance Meditation Mystery School, facilitating thousands of healings, soul awakenings and journeys throughout the world. The core pillars—*The Daughters of Miracles—Daughters of Miriam, The Kingship of Illumination, Radiance Healer Certification Program, Radiance Tree of Life Master Course* and the *Radiance Pure Energy* at-home study course/guide, a pathway for all people to experience the mystical energy knowledge of Light.

www.deirdrehade.com

www.thefoundationforradiance.org

roshi joan halifax

Roshi Joan Halifax, Ph.D., is a Buddhist teacher, Zen priest, anthropologist and pioneer in the field of end-of-life care. She is founder, abbot and head teacher of the Upaya Institute and Zen Center in Santa Fe, N.M. She received a National Science Foundation Fellowship in Visual Anthropology, was an Honorary Research Fellow in Medical Ethnobotany at Harvard University and is a Distinguished Visiting Scholar at the Library of Congress. She is a founding teacher of the Zen Peacemaker Orde and her work and practice for more than four decades has focused on applied Buddhism. Her books include: *The Human Encounter with Death (with Stanislav Grof); The Fruitful Darkness; Simplicity in the Complex: A Buddhist Life in America; Being with Dying: Cultivating Compassion and Wisdom in the Presence of Death; Being with Dying: Compassionate End-of-Life Care (Professional Training Guide)* and *Being with Dying: Cultivating Compassion and Fearlessness in the Presence of Death.* She is a Lindisfarne Fellow, co-director of the Fellowship and a Mind and Life Board member.
www.upaya.org

gina rose halpern

Rev. Gina Rose Halpern D.Min., BCCC, is the founder of the Chaplaincy Institute, an Interfaith Seminary in Berkeley, Calif. She has dedicated her life to Interfaith and inclusive education. As a chaplain, artist and teacher, she has practiced creative ways to serve across divides and provide compassionate care. She is the author and illustrator of *Where is Tibet?* and *To Heal the Broken Heart.*
www.chaplaincyinstitute.org

andrew harvey

Andrew Harvey is the founder and director of the Institute of Sacred Activism, an international organization that invites concerned people to take up the challenge of our contemporary global crises by becoming inspired and effective agents of change. Sacred activism is a form of compassion-in-action that is born of a fusion of deep spiritual passion with wise radical action in the world. The large-scale practice of sacred activism can become an essential force for preserving and healing the planet and its inhabitants. Andrew Harvey has taught at Oxford and Cornell Universities as well as various colleges and spiritual centers throughout the world. He has written over thirty books.

www.andrewharvey.net

sandra ingerman

Sandra Ingerman, MA, is a world-renowned teacher of shamanism. She is recognized for bringing ancient cross-cultural healing methods into our modern culture, and addressing the needs of our times. A licensed therapist, she is the author of eight books, including *Soul Retrieval, Medicine for the Earth, Shamanic Journeying, How to Heal Toxic Thoughts, How to Thrive in Changing Times* and *Awakening to the Spirit World*. She is also the author of seven CD programs produced by Sounds True.

www.sandraingerman.com.

eli jaxon-bear

In 1990 Eli Jaxon-Bear met his final teacher, Sri H.W.L. Poonja, in Lucknow, India. Confirming Eli's realization, his teacher sent him back into the world to share his unique psychological insights into the nature of egoic suffering in support of self-realization. He dedicates his life to passing on the transmission of his teacher. Eli Jaxon-Bear is the author of *Sudden Awakening*; *The Enneagram of Liberation: From Fixation to Freedom* and is the editor of *Wake Up and Roar: Satsang with H.W.L. Poonja*. Eli currently meets people and teaches through the Leela Foundation, a nonprofit organization dedicated to world peace and freedom through universal self-realization.

www.leela.org

kathleen jenks

Kathleen Jenks is the author of the autobiographical *Journey of a Dream Animal*; *The River and the Stone,* an historical novel about Moses, Miriam and Aaron in ancient Egypt; and the *Green World Oracle*. She has a Ph.D. in religious studies from the University of California, Santa Barbara. For nine years she taught courses on mythology and ritual at Pacifica Graduate Institute. She has guided private and group reincarnation sessions since 1973. She currently teaches in local colleges and lives and writes in her ivy-covered house, "Green Man Abbey."

www.mythinglinks.org

Chan Master Guo Jun is currently the abbot of Mahabodhi Monastery in Singapore and teaches internationally. He is Chan Master Sheng Yen's youngest dharma heir, and served as abbot of Sheng Yen's Pine Bush, N.Y., retreat center from 2005 to 2008. Guo Jun holds undergraduate degrees in biotechnology, psychology and sociology, as well as a Master's degree in Buddhist studies. A native of Singapore, he received his full monastic ordination in Taiwan. He is a lineage holder and successor in Chan as well as the Xianshou and Cien schools of Chinese Buddhism, and is the author of *Essential Chan Buddhism: The Character and Spirit of Chinese Zen.*
www.putige.org

Cynthia Jurs is a teacher of sacred activism and engaged Buddhism in the lineage of Thich Nhat Hanh. In 1990, on pilgrimage in Nepal, she met a one-hundred-and-six-year-old lama named Charok Rinpoche living in a remote cave, from whom she received the practice of the *Earth Treasure Vases*. For over twenty years she has traveled to diverse cultures around the world facilitating collaborations with young activists and indigenous elders in a unique ritual that strengthens community and catalyzes solutions to the planet's problems. She founded Alliance for the Earth, a nonprofit organization dedicated to supporting the emergence of a global community committed to planetary healing and collective awakening. She directs the Open Way Sangha in New Mexico.
www.earthtreasurevase.org

jyoti

Jyoti is an internationally renowned spiritual advisor with a Ph.D. in transpersonal psychology, who also completed postgraduate study at the C.G. Jung Institute in Zurich, Switzerland. She is one of the founders of Kayumari, a spiritual healing community located in North America, Europe and Brazil. She is the spiritual director of the Center for Sacred Studies, a 501(c)3 organization dedicated to sustaining a way of life based on collaboration and reciprocity with the Earth and all Her beings. Jyoti has devoted her life to a prayer of unity on the planet, developing alliances through collaborative relationships with those dedicated to the Earth and Her sustainability.

www.sacredstudies.org
www.grandmotherscouncil.org

tamam kahn

Tamam Kahn is a senior teacher in the Sufi Ruhaniat International and is married to Pir Shabda Kahn. Her book, *Untold: A History of the Wives of Prophet Muhammad* (Monkfish Book Publishing Co.), received an International Book Award for 2011. Tamam's next book is on Fatima, daughter of the Prophet Muhammad. She presents her findings on early women of Islam at conferences and Sufi gatherings. In 2009 she was invited to recite her poetry at an International Sufi Conference in Marrakech, Morocco. She studied with Tai Situ Rinpoche and served on his board at the Maitreya Institute in San Francisco.

www.completeword.com

gloria karpinski

Gloria D. Karpinski is a holistic counselor, spiritual director, teacher and author. Her seminars as well as her individual in-depth life attunements emphasize the relevancy of universal spiritual principles to everyday life and the inter dynamics of mind, body, emotions and spirit. Gloria is the author of *Where Two Worlds Touch: Spiritual Rites of Passage* and *Barefoot on Holy Ground: Twelve Lessons in Spiritual Craftsmanship*, both published by Ballantine Books. Gloria lives in Winston-Salem, North Carolina. Her web site includes a calendar of her workshops, lectures, intensives and other specialized programs. www.gloriakarpinski.com

byron katie

Byron Katie's simple yet powerful method of inquiry into the cause of all suffering is called The Work. Since 1986, she has introduced The Work to millions of people throughout the world. Eckhart Tolle calls The Work "a great blessing for our planet," and *Time* magazine named Katie a "spiritual innovator for the new millennium." She has written several books, including the bestsellers *Loving What Is, I Need Your Love—Is That True?* and *A Thousand Names for Joy*; as well as *Question Your Thinking—Change the World, Who Would You Be Without Your Story?, A Friendly Universe* and, for children, *Tiger-Tiger, Is It True?* Her website features many free materials to download, as well as audio and video clips, a schedule of events and a free helpline with a network of The Work facilitators. www.thework.com

william keepin

William Keepin, Ph.D., is cofounder of Satyana Institute and Gender Reconciliation International. He works in partnership with the Desmond and Leah Tutu Legacy Foundation and has convened eighty programs in eight countries for reconciliation between women and men. Will has practiced silent meditation for thirty years and leads retreats bringing contemplative spiritual leaders together from across the major religions, including the *Dawn of Interspirituality* conference. He is a physicist and former whistleblower in nuclear science policy. His books include *Divine Duality: The Power of Reconciliation Between Women and Men* and *Song of the Earth: A Synthesis of Scientific and Spiritual Worldviews*.
www.satyana.org
www.grworld.org.

colleen kelley

Colleen Kelley is an artist, poet and teacher. She is currently working on a series titled "I Nurse the Milk of Millenia" and a multimedia performance with electric cello played by Jami Sieber, rooted in their experiences with the Asian Elephants of India and Thailand. She was the art director, visionary and co-author for ten years on *The Box: Remembering the Gift*. This collaborative project resulted in a series of three books and artifacts contained in a wooden box. It is an environmental curriculum that is being used by groups and individuals around the world.
www.colleen-kelley.com

Ruth King is an insight meditation teacher and emotional wisdom author and consultant. Ruth has a Masters in clinical psychology and is a graduate of Spirit Rock Meditation Center's Dedicated Practitioner Program and a guiding teacher at Insight Meditation Community of Washington, D.C. She is the author of *Healing Rage: Women Making Inner Peace Possible,* and designed *The Emotional Wisdom Cards* as well as the *Mindful of Race Retreat: A Stimulus for Social Healing and Leadership* and the *Mindfulness Practices for Living Well* course. She is the founder of Mindful Members, a meditation practice community in Charlotte, N.C., where she resides.
www.ruthking.net

Tito La Rosa, a descendent of the Quechua Indians of the Peruvian Andes, has spent more than a decade recovering and preserving, studying and intuiting the ancestral music of Peru. Tito is a *curandero de sonido*—a sound healer. When performing ritual and ceremony for healing, he enters into parallel worlds to bring forth sound that elevates the vibration of an individual and allows for healing and balance to occur. Tito was asked by the Peruvian Institute of Culture to play two-thousand-year-old instruments at the Museum of the Lord of Sipan to reinvent the sounds these instruments made. In recreating the sounds of this culture that had disappeared into time, Tito stated, "Time, like death, is a lie."
www.titolarosa.net

gail larsen

Gail Larsen has led a life of sufficient adventure to behoove her to learn to pray, with a path informed by studies in shamanism and angel guidance. She is the founder of Real Speaking® and author of *Transformational Speaking: If You Want to Change the World, Tell a Better Story.* She lives in Santa Fe, N.M.

www.realspeaking.com

robin lim

Robin Lim, CPM, was born in 1956, the offspring of a Filipino-Chinese woman and a German, Irish, Native American man. Together, her parents built a bridge of love across cultures. She now lives in Indonesia, where she is called "Ibu Robin" (Mother Robin). Lim is a certified professional midwife with the North American Registry of Midwives and Ikatan Bidan Indonesia. She devotes her life to Yayasan Bumi Sehat, a not-for-profit organization with clinics in Bali and Aceh. Along with receiving babies into the world, Ibu Robin is a doula and the author of several books on childbirth, in both English and Bahasa Indonesia. Her book of poetry, *The Geometry of Splitting Souls,* was released by Blue Light Press/!st World Library. Robin's two new books have been released in the Philippines: *Butterfly People*, a novel, and *Placenta... the Forgotten Chakra*, which promises to make gentle birth more gentle.

Robin's support and inspiration is her family—her husband Wil and their eight astounding children. She is *Lola* for three grandchildren: Zhòuie, Bodhi and Tashi.

In 2006 Ibu Robin received the Alexander Langer Peace Award in Italy. In 2011 she was named CNN Hero of the Year for her work in maternal and child health in Indonesia and disaster zones. Her religion is Gratitude.

www.robinlimsupport.org

arvol looking horse

Chief Arvol Looking Horse was born on the Cheyenne River reservation in South Dakota in 1954. At the age of twelve he was given the enormous responsibility of becoming the nineteenth-generation Keeper of the Sacred White Buffalo Calf Pipe. He was raised in an era that gave witness to the suppression of his peoples spiritual practices. He says he decided to "work for change and let the world know how beautiful our way of life is, so the Seventh Generation can have a better life." His life has revolved around his commitment to work towards religious freedom and cultural survival and revival.

www.wodakota.org

peter makena

Peter Makena learned with Sufi teachers the use of the voice in songs, chants and prayer. Today, Peter leads singing groups and facilitates countless gatherings, joining people in song and prayer to create "meetings of the heart." The greatest influences on his work with voice and presence were Sufi meditations and chants, as well as Indian kirtan and ghazal-style songs. For four years Peter led daily singing groups in a meditation ashram in India. He lives in northern California and is on tour at yoga and meditation centers, music festivals and meditation retreats throughout the United States and in Europe. Peter has published nine CDs of his music.

www.petermankena.com
www.makenasinging.com

trevor malkinson

Trevor Malkinson grew up in Victoria, B.C., Canada, and completed an undergraduate degree in philosophy at the University of Victoria and a graduate degree in philosophy at Brock University. He is currently working on a Masters of Divinity at Vancouver School of Theology, and is training to be a minister in the United Church of Canada.

www.beamsandstruts.com

brigitte mars

Brigitte Mars is a professional member of the American Herbalist Guild and has worked with natural medicine as a nutritional consultant for over 40 years. She teaches herbal medicine at Naropa University, Bauman College of Holistic Nutrition, the School of Natural Medicine and Just for Health School of Herbalism. She has taught at Omega Institute, Esalen, Kripalu and the Mayo Clinic. She blogs for the Huffington Post and Care2. Brigitte is the author of fourteen books, including *The Country Almanac of Home Remedies, The Desktop Guide to Herbal Medicine, Beauty by Nature, Addiction Free Naturally, The Sexual Herbal, Healing Herbal Teas* and *Rawsome!*. Her latest project is a phone app called *IPlant*.

www.brigittemars.com

Rainbeau Mars uses literature, song, theatrical expression and activism to spread knowledge, power and inspiration throughout the world. She has made a variety of cinematic appearances, taken community leadership roles and been involved with literary features. Since writing her first book, *28 Days to Your Superstar Glow*, she has been striving to express and create. Through these outlets, her true passion and purpose becomes transparent. Her journey is an invitation to all who desire expansion and transformation mentally, physically and spiritually. In the name of health and happiness, her dedication to service is an offering of empowerment and fulfillment. www.rainbeaumars.com

david mccallum

David McCallum, S.J. is a Jesuit priest, educator and spiritual director. He has a doctorate in adult learning and leadership from Columbia University and works in the area of adult spiritual maturation, leadership and organizational development and mission integration. Currently, he serves as the chief mission officer of Le Moyne College in Syracuse, N.Y.

father william hart mcnichols

William Hart McNichols has been "drawing and coloring in his room" since he was five years old. He was a member of the Society of Jesus (the Jesuits) from 1968 to 2002. He studied philosophy, theo-logy and art at St. Louis University, Boston College, Boston University and Weston School of Theology in Cambridge, Mass. Father Bill furthered his art studies at California College of Arts and Crafts in Oakland in 1977. He was ordained as a Roman Catholic priest in Denver on May 25, 1979. In 1983 he received an MFA in landscape painting from Pratt Institute in Brooklyn, N.Y. From 1983 to 1990 he worked with the AIDS Hospice team of St. Vincent's Hospital in Manhattan, N.Y. During that time, he also illustrated twenty-five books, mostly children's books, for the Paulist Press. In 1990, he moved to Albuquerque, N.M. to study the technique, history and spirituality of icon painting with Russian-American master painter Robert Lentz. Father Bill also assists with sacramental ministry in the Archdiocese of Santa Fe, N.M. In 2007, Father Bill began to work on the Publication Ministry of the Icons. In 2008 to 2009 his first icon exhibit, *Silence of the Storm: Icons and Images*, featuring twenty-six originals, was shown at the Millicent Rogers Museum in Taos, N.M. Currently several originals and many reproductions of his work are on exhibit at Solstice Gallery in Taos, N.M.

www.fatherbill.org

dunya dianne mcpherson

Dunya Dianne McPherson is an acclaimed authority and meditative leader and the founder and principal teacher of the healing movement system, Dancemeditation™, a path of breath and intuition. Dunya is a Juilliard graduate, Sufi Master and National Endowment for the Arts Choreography Fellow. Dunya's teaching credits include Princeton University, Swarthmore College, New York University, Barnard College, New York Open Center, Kripalu Center for Yoga and Netherlands Mystik Festival. Dunya holds a Master's in writing and is the author of *Skin of Glass: Finding Spirit in the Flesh*, a memoir about dance as a spiritual path.

www.dancemeditation.org

dan millman

Dan Millman, a former world champion athlete, coach, martial arts instructor and college professor, is the author of *Way of the Peaceful Warrior* (adapted to film in 2006) and fifteen other books read by millions of people in twenty-nine languages. Dan teaches worldwide and has influenced people from all walks of life, including leaders in the fields of health, psychology, education, business, politics, sports, entertainment and the arts.

www.peacefulwarrior.com

arnold mindell

Dr. Arnold Mindell is best known for his development and application of Process Work and for the 20 books that he has written and published on the subject. He is one of the founding members of the Process Work Institute in Portland, Ore., and the Research Society for Process Oriented Psychology in Zurich, Switzerland. Along with his wife, Amy Mindell, he offers extensive teaching, training, facilitation and consultation in Process Work, which is a wide-spectrum approach to individual, organizational and global problems. Arnold is a regular keynote speaker at international conferences and an international teacher, trainer, facilitator and advisor. He also works in private practice as a therapist in Portland, Ore., and he is an avid researcher, skier, runner and hiker.

www.aamindell.net

devaa haley mitchell

Rev. Dr. Devaa Haley Mitchell is a transformational leader who supports people to reconnect with their spiritual depths, unleash their leadership gifts and step into their full potential. She is cofounder of the Shift Network and founder of the Inspiring Women Summit, a community of over 70,000 women from more than one hundred and sixty countries. Through the Soulful Women Wisdom School, she offers deeply experiential and transformative programs that guide hundreds of women to connect more deeply with spirit. As a musician, Devaa fuses East and West with sensuous, danceable tunes. Her debut album, *Sacred Alchemy*, aims to reawaken and liberate the many dimensions of the sacred feminine.

www.devaa.com
www.inspiringwomensummit.com
www.soulfulwomen.com

n. scott momaday

N. Scott Momaday was born in 1934 in Lawton, Okla., to a Kiowa father and Cherokee/mixed-blood mother. In the course of his career, he has received numerous awards, including the Pulitzer Prize for Fiction, the Academy of American Poets Prize, the National Medal of Arts and the Premio Letterario Internazionale Mondello, Italy's highest literary honor. Momaday lives in Santa Fe, N.M.

Rev. Dr. Swan (Sahra Renata) is an author, poet and artist, a visionary and a mystic, with an M.A. in spiritual philosophy and a Ph.D. in metaphysics. She is an initiate of the highest ancient mystery schools and an extraordinary healer who is able to merge her consciousness with many dimensions and realities. Her divine sacred wall-hangings, known as Temple Veils, are made from antique eastern silks, jewels and crystals. She writes sacred poetry about divine mystery and love, shortly available on CD. She is author of the quartet *The Book of Sahra, Jesus' Secret Wife* and *Poems of the Golden Rose*. www.bookofsahra.com

Oriah is the author of the international best-selling books: *The Invitation, The Dance* and *The Call*. Her much-loved poem "The Invitation" has been shared around the world. Trained in a shamanic tradition, her medicine name, "Mountain Dreamer," means "one who likes to find and push the edge." Using story, poetry and shamanic ceremony, deeply personal writing and work as a group facilitator and spiritual mentor, Oriah explores how to follow the thread of our heart's longing into a life where we can choose joy without denying the challenges of a human life. www.oriah.org

Caroline Muir is an educator and the author of two bestselling books, *Tantra Goddess: A Memoir of Sexual Awakening* and *Tantra: The Art of Conscious Loving*, co-authored with Charles Muir. Caroline founded the Divine Feminine Awakening Immersion in 2005. She uncovered "the missing piece in modern sexuality": the Ah. The Practice of Ah

is a full-spectrum, feminine-wisdom approach to sexual healing and awakening for men and women. Ah invites us to elevate out of our animal nature and into lovers who regard and revere the body as a home for the spirit. Caroline believes that education at every age is at the core of what advances human existence.
www.divine-feminine.com

millard murphy

Millard Murphy was a founding member of the intentional community La Tierra in Sebastopol, Calif., where he has lived since 1989. He has been a practicing lawyer and law school professor since 1986 in the arena of civil and human rights for prisoners, teaching law students how to provide legal services to prisoners in civil rights matters. Born in Los Angeles, he has remained close to home in California with his wife, Laurel, of thirty-two years, and his thirty-one-year-old son lives nearby.

ravi nathwani

Ravi Nathwani was born in East Africa and raised in India in the Hindu tradition. He lectures and leads workshops on Patanjali's Yoga Sutras and the Bhagavad Gita for Yoga Teacher Trainings in the United States and Mexico. Ravi has taught at Tufts University since 1998, and also teaches at the College of Marin and JFK University in California. He also leads satsangs, meditation groups and workshops on a variety of Vedic/Yoga topics. Ravi has an MBA from Boston University and has lived in Bombay, London, Boston, San Francisco and Mexico.

hella neumann

Hella Neumann earned her Master's in art and education from the University of Berlin. In 1975 she founded Atelier Unterm Dach Art School in Germany, and directed the school for eighteen years. Her work included meditation, art therapy, bio-energetics and the biodynamic massage of Gerda Boyesen, London. In 1994 she began intensive study of systemic constellation work in Germany with the founder Bert Hellinger. She began her own constellation work in 1997 under the name "Songs of the Ancestors," leading family constellation workshops, doing private constellations and training facilitators. She attends the national and international conferences in Germany and the United States.
www.songsoftheancestors.com

wallace j. nichols

Dr. Wallace J. Nichols is a research associate at California Academy of Sciences. He earned his Bachelors in biology and Spanish from DePauw University, an MEM in environmental policy and economics from Duke University and a Ph.D. in wildlife ecology and evolutionary biology from the University of Arizona.

Dr. Nichols has authored over one hundred scientific publications and reports on ocean conservation science, mentors a motivated group of international graduate students and advises numerous boards and committees as part of a commitment to building a stronger, more progressive, connected environmental community. Currently, he's also working on BlueMind, bringing neuroscience to our understanding of the benefits of healthy waterway in our lives and a book on the subject with Little, Brown & Company. He lives on California's SLOWCOAST with his family.
www.wallacejnichols.org

christa obuchowski

Christa J. Obuchowski is a traditional naturopath, botanical perfumer, distiller and educator. In 1994, Christa founded the AromaBotanica Institute in Santa Fe, N.M. She teaches classes on plant medicine, the art of perfume-making and self-care. Growing up in Germany, Christa was first introduced to plants at a young age, helping her grandfather make plant medicines, tinctures and sauerkraut. She studied aromatherapy, plant medicine and distillation with leading authorities in the field. Among her varied experiences are biodynamic gardening and studying with Mayan healers in Belize. She travels the world to learn about plants, extracts, scent and incense.

www.christajobuchowski.com
www.aromabotanica.com

james o'dea

James O'Dea is the award-winning author of *Cultivating Peace, Creative Stress* and other works, and the lead faculty for the Shift Network's acclaimed Peace Ambassador Training program. He has conducted frontline social-healing dialogues for many years. James is the former president of the Institute of Noetic Sciences in Washington, D.C., a past office director of Amnesty International and the former CEO of the Seva Foundation. He offers consulting and leadership intensives at his mountain home in Crestone, Colo.

www.jamesodea.com

Richard Packham was born into a devout Mormon family and was raised in that religion. He married his Mormon high school sweetheart, graduated from Brigham Young University and began to raise a family. In his late twenties, as a graduate student, he began to question Mormon claims, and after three years of research he came to the conclusion that those claims were false. His leaving the Mormon Church led to his wife divorcing him. After studying many other religions, Richard came to the conclusion that their supernatural claims were false, although many had useful and humane teachings that could prove to be valuable guides for life. He realized then that he was an atheist. In 2001, he founded the Exmormon Foundation, which helps to disseminate more accurate information about Mormonism than is usually available from official Mormon sources. He spent his professional life as a college teacher, mostly in San Francisco, teaching foreign languages and computer science. He also holds a law degree and has practiced law. He is now retired and lives on a ranch in Oregon, raising timber and cattle with his present wife of forty years. He is also active in the online ex-Mormon community.
www.packham.n4m.org

Cofounder of *New Earth Records*, Waduda studied psychology at the University of Rome, where she became a regular contributor to the hugely popular *Radio Donna*, Italy's first and only feminist radio station. She gives ongoing seminars and lectures on the subject of hypnosis and meditation for transformation and contributes regularly to various Italian magazines on the subjects of wellness, music and Eastern philosophy. She lives in the wilderness of Northern New Mexico with her beloved Bhikkhu, and travels to India and around the world regularly. www.newearthrecords.com

robert peng

Robert Peng is the founder of Elixir Light Qigong. He began his qigong apprenticeship with the legendary monk Xiao Yao when he was a boy. As part of his training he did a hundred-day water fast in a dark, underground chamber. From this experience Peng developed the ability to discharge a powerful, concentrated form of Qi ("bioenergy") that feels like a strong electric current. Today he uses this extraordinary power to heal and inspire. Peng teaches internationally, is the author of *The Master Key: The Qigong Way to Unlock Your Hidden Power* and producer of *The Master Key Companion* CD and DVD series.
www.robertpeng.com

tom pinkson

Tom Pinkson, Ph.D., is a psychologist, author, musician, ceremonial retreat and vision-fast leader and sacred storyteller who helped start the first at-home hospice in the United States, then worked with terminally ill children at the Center for Attitudinal Healing in California for thirty-two years. His new book, *Fruitful Aging: Finding the Gold in the Golden Years*, is about meeting the challenges of aging in a skillful manner, growing this time of life into the richest and most rewarding time of all. Tom is a bridge builder, translating indigenous wisdom ways to help people wake up and connect to deeper, authentic being, exploring how to live, love and work from the holy place of soul.
www.drtompinkson.com
www.nierica.com

kristena prater

Kristena Prater is a humanitarian activist and wellness consultant working with people to turn troubles into triumph. She believes in prayer as affirmation, which can be integrated into any religion. As the head of the Tessa Foundation, named in honor of Kristena's daughter, who passed away in 2006, she has helped people in Tonga, Nepal, Guatemala, Colorado and New Mexico plant seeds of sustainable life. Her poems and articles have been published in various periodicals and she is currently working on a book and a screenplay. She is a mother of four and lives between Santa Fe, N.M., and Aspen, Colo.

www.tessafoundation.org

www.kristenaprater.com.

sri prem baba

Sri Prem Baba is a Brazilian master teacher in the Sachcha spiritual lineage of northern India. He offers a method of self-discovery he calls "The Path of the Heart," which bridges psychology and spirituality, East and West, the Amazon and the Himalayas. Prem Baba resides five months a year in India, where he teaches through daily *satsangs* (wisdom talks). Path of the Heart retreats and workshops are offered throughout the world. His latest book is *From Suffering to Joy: The Path of the Heart.*

www.pathheart.org

deva premal & miten

Deva Premal & Miten began their journey into love and music in 1990 when they met in India at the ashram of the controversial mystic, Osho. They see themselves as part of a 5,000-year-old tradition of mantra practice. Their worldwide concerts and bestselling albums have introduced millions to the benefits of chanting mantras from sacred Sanskrit texts. H.H. the Dalai Lama is known to use their music for his personal enjoyment and Rock icon Cher covered their famous adaption of the Gayatri Mantra on her Farewell Tour Movie. Eckhart Tolle says of their music, "...it is Pure Magic...!"
www.devapremalmiten.com

imam jamal rahman

Imam Jamal Rahman is a popular speaker on Islam, Sufi spirituality and interfaith relations. Cofounder and Muslim Sufi minister at Seattle's Interfaith Community Sanctuary and adjunct faculty at Seattle University, Jamal travels nationally and internationally, presenting at retreats and workshops. He is the author of several books, including *Spiritual Gems of Islam: Insights & Practices from the Qur'an, Hadith, Rumi & Muslim Teaching Stories to Enlighten the Heart & Mind*. Since 9/11 Jamal has been collaborating with Rabbi Ted Falcon and Pastor Don Mackenzie. Affectionately known as the Interfaith Amigos, they tour the country sharing the message of spiritual inclusivity.
www.jamalrahman.com
www.interfaithcommunitysanctuary.org
www.interfaithamigos.com

father richard rohr

Father Richard Rohr is a globally recognized ecumenical teacher bearing witness to the universal awakening within Christian mysticism and the Perennial Tradition. He is a Franciscan priest of the New Mexico Province and founder of the Center for Action and Contemplation (CAC) in Albuquerque, N.M. Father Richard's teaching is grounded in the Franciscan alternative orthodoxy, including practices of contemplation and lived kenosis (self-emptying), which expresses itself in radical compassion, particularly for the socially marginalized. Father Richard is author of numerous books, including *Everything Belongs*, *Adam's Return*, *The Naked Now*, *Breathing Under Water*, *Falling Upward* and *Immortal Diamond: The Search for Our True Self.*

CAC is home to the Rohr Institute where Father Richard is academic dean of the Living School for Action and Contemplation. Drawing upon Christianity's place within the Perennial Tradition, the mission of the Rohr Institute is to produce compassionate and powerfully learned individuals who will work for positive change in the world based on awareness of our common union with God and all beings. Learn more about Father Richard and CAC at cac.org.

kim rosen

Kim Rosen, MFA, is the author of *Saved by a Poem: The Transformative Power of Words.* In the darkest moment of her life, when psychological and spiritual teachings could not reach her, she found poetry. Now she combines her love of speaking poems with her background in spirituality and psychotherapy, offering poetry as a transformative agent for individuals and communities throughout the world. She is the co-creator of four CDs and her work has been featured in *O, The Sun, The New Yorker* and *Spirituality & Health* magazines, among other publications.

www.kimrosen.net

peter russell

Author and public speaker Peter Russell is recognized as one of the leading thinkers on consciousness and contemporary spirituality. His books include *The Global Brain, Waking Up in Time* and *From Science to God,* and his video, *The Global Brain,* won international acclaim. Peter believes that the critical challenge today is to free human thinking from the limited beliefs and attitudes that lie behind so many of our problems—personal, social and global.
www.peterrussell.com

regina sara ryan

Regina Sara Ryan, the author of *Praying Dangerously* and *The Woman Awake,* is a former Catholic nun, who has studied contemplation for over forty years. After leaving the convent in the early 1970s, Regina explored other religious traditions and was inspired by the lives of the great mystics and sages of Hinduism, Christianity, Buddhism and Sufism. Since meeting her own spiritual teacher, the Western Baul master Lee Lozowick, in 1984, Regina continues to follow what she calls a path of "unashamed devotion" in which she works to bring her life of contemplation into action.
www.reginasararyan.com

bruce sanguin

Bruce Sanguin is an ordained minister in the United Church of Canada, having served congregations for the past twenty-seven years. Today he lives in Vancouver, British Columbia, writing, speaking, on the life and practice of evolutionary mysticism. He is the author of five books, including *If Darwin Prayed: Prayers for Evolutionary Mystics*, which won the IPPY gold medal award for the best spiritual book of 2012. His latest is *The Advance of Love: Reading the Bible With An Evolutionary Heart.*
www.brucesanguin.com

Rabbi Zalman Schachter-Shalomi, author of *Paradigm Shift, From Age-ing to Sage-ing, Wrapped in a Holy Flame* and *Jewish With Feeling*, is professor emeritus at Temple University and past holder of the World Wisdom Chair at Naropa University. He is the founder of ALEPH, Alliance for Jewish Renewal and is Spiritual Director of YESOD, Foundation for a Jewish Future. Read more about Reb Zalman at the Reb Zalman Legacy Project website. www.rzlp.org

nicki scully

Nicki Scully has been teaching healing, shamanic arts and the Egyptian Mysteries since 1983. Techniques from her alchemical healing form are used internationally by thousands of practitioners. In the late 1980s, Nicki founded Shamanic Journeys, Ltd., which specializes in spiritual pilgrimages to Egypt, retreats and teleweb classes. Her latest book is *Planetary Healing: Spirit Medicine for Global Transformation,* which was co-written with her husband, Mark Hallert, and is part of a trilogy including *Alchemical Healing: A Guide to Spiritual, Physical and Transformational Medicine* and *Power Animal Meditations.* Nicki lives in Eugene, Ore., where she maintains a comprehensive healing and shamanic consulting practice. www.shamanicjourneys.com

rabbi rami shapiro

Rabbi Rami Shapiro, Ph.D., an award-winning author, poet, essayist and educator, is cofounder of One River Wisdom School in Sewanee, TN (oneriverwisdomschool.com). The author of over twenty-four books on religion and spirituality, Rami also writes a regular column for *Spirituality and Health* magazine called *Roadside Assistance for the Spiritual Traveler*. His most recent books are *Perennial Wisdom for the Spiritually Independent* (Skylight Paths) and a series of short e-books called *Rabbi Rami Guides*. www.rabbirami.com

joanne shenandoah

Joanne Shenandoah, Ph.D., is one of America's most celebrated and critically acclaimed musicians. She is a Grammy Award winner, with over forty music awards (including a record thirteen Native American Music awards) and sixteen recordings. She has captured the hearts of audiences all over the world, from North and South America, South Africa, Europe, Australia and Korea, with praise for her work to promote universal peace. She is a board member of the Hiawatha Institute for Indigenous Knowledge.

Joanne and her daughter Leah recorded on the title track "Path to Zero" with Jim Morrison, which also included the artists Sting, Bono, Sinead O'Conner, Robert Downey, Jr., and others.

Joanne has performed for His Holiness the Dalai Lama and at St. Peter's at the Vatican in Italy, where she performed an original composition for the celebration for the canonization of the first Native American Saint Kateri Tekakwitha. Shenandoah has performed at prestigious events such as the White House, Carnegie Hall, five Presidential inaugurations, Madison Square Garden, Crystal Bridges Museum, the NMAI-Smithsonian, the Ordway Theater, Hummingbird Centre, Toronto Skydome, the Parliament of the Worlds Religions (Africa, Spain and Australia) and Woodstock 1994. www.hiawatha.syr.edu

Nina Simons is cofounder and co-CEO of the nonprofit Bioneers, an organization that since 1990 has identified, featured and disseminated breakthrough solutions for people and planet. She co-facilitates Cultivating Women's Leadership retreats with Toby Herzlich and co-edited the recently published *Moonrise: The Power of Women Leading from the Heart*. She was previously president of Seeds of Change and strategic marketing director with Odwalla and lives outside Santa Fe, N.M., with her husband and partner. www.bioneers.org

Visionary artist Susan Slotter—photographer, filmmaker, writer and integrative creative midwife—left the corporate world in 1989 to follow a call. She is the creator of *SoulScapes®*, experiences that connect us to the divine presence within ourselves, our relationships and the world around us. Called "portals into consciousness," *SoulScapes* images, films, portraits and workshop experiences are tools for personal and collective transformation. *SoulScapes* have been presented through venues such as the Omega Institute, Fetzer Institute and Institute of Noetic Sciences; magazines including *The Sun* magazine, *Yoga Journal, Gnosis, Creation Spirituality, Camera and Darkroom, Popular Photography* and *Photo District News*; the Maine and Santa Fe Photographic Workshops and Hasselblad USA. Susan has created award-winning short films, worked on independent feature documentaries and has been developing an "evocumentary" on broadening ideas about leadership from the heart of the collective. www.susanslotter.com

huston smith

Huston Smith is Thomas J. Watson Professor of Religion and Distinguished Adjunct Professor of Philosophy, Emeritus, at Syracuse University. For fifteen years he was Professor of Philosophy at the Massachusetts Institute of Technology and for a decade before that he taught at Washington University in Saint Louis. Most recently he has served as Visiting Professor of Religious Studies at the University of California, Berkeley. Smith is the holder of twelve honorary degrees. His fourteen books include *The World's Religions* and *Why Religion Matters*. In 1996 Bill Moyers devoted a five-part PBS special, "The Wisdom of Faith with Huston Smith," to his life and work. His film documentaries on Hinduism, Tibetan Buddhism and Sufism have all won international awards and *The Journal of Ethnomusicology* lauded his discovery of Tibetan multiphonic chanting as "an important landmark in the study of music."

jeff sollins

Jeff is the founder of Bridges In Medicine. He received his medical degree from the University of Maryland School of Medicine, where he completed a three-year residency in internal medicine. Board Certified and Diplomat of the American Board of Integrative Holistic Medicine, he also served on the board for over a decade. As a member of the American College of Physicians and Society of Internal Medicine, he has managed emergency rooms and multi-specialty practices. Jeff's loves include music composition and performing, Shotokan Karate, prayer, his mystical animals and, of course, his amazing miracle wife.
www.bridgesinmedicine.com

sobonfu somé

Sobonfu Somé is a respected lecturer and author. As the founder of Wisdom Spring, Inc., an organization dedicated to the preservation and sharing of indigenous wisdom and fundraising for wells, schools and health projects in Africa, she is one of the foremost voices of African spirituality to come to the West, bringing insights and healing gifts from her West African culture to this one. Sobonfu tours the United States and Europe teaching workshops. Her books include: *The Spirit of Intimacy, Welcoming Spirit Home* and *Falling out of Grace*.
www.sobonfu.com
www.wisdomspring.org

tara stapleton

Tara is originally from Chicago, and has lived in several countries, participating in and learning about various cultures and traditions. She has spent decades studying and practicing Tibetan Buddhism. After many years of solitude and meditation, she continues to apply what she learns from the Heart Essence of the Masters into her everyday life and healing practice. Tara incorporates wisdom from those various spiritual traditions, along with shamanism and astrology, into her worldview. In 2010, she created The Prayerfield of the Heart Essence project, a vast collective of enlightened beings from the spiritual realms whose purpose is assisting humanity and all sentient beings in personal and collective healing, growth and evolution. Tara lives and has her healing practice as an energy worker, medium and astrologer in Santa Fe, N.M. She also teaches Sky Dancing, a form of spiritual dance and meditation and is presently writing and bringing through a form of Dakini yoga.
www.prayerfieldoftheheartessence.org

margaret starbird

Margaret Starbird holds B.A. and M.A. degrees from the University of Maryland and pursued graduate studies at Vanderbilt Divinity School. She is the author of several widely acclaimed books reclaiming Mary Magdalene and the Sacred Feminine in Christianity. Starbird gives lectures and retreats worldwide and has appeared in numerous TV documentaries. Her books include *The Woman with the Alabaster Jar* and *The Goddess in the Gospels*, both mentioned in *The Da Vinci Code*, followed by *Mary Magdalene, Bride in Exile*. Other titles include *Magdalene's Lost Legacy* and *The Tarot Trumps and the Holy Grail*. Married with five grown children, Margaret lives near Seattle. www.margaretstarbird.net

mirabai starr

Mirabai Starr is a critically acclaimed author and translator of sacred literature. She teaches and speaks widely on contemplative practice, interspiritual experience and the transformational power of loss. Her works include *Dark Night of the Soul* by John of the Cross. *The Interior Castle* and *The Book of My Life* by Teresa of Avila, *The Showings* of *Julian of Norwich, Mother of God Similar to Fire* (in collaboration with iconographer, William Hart McNichols) and *Contemplations and Living Wisdom* (Sounds True). *GOD OF LOVE: A Guide to the Heart of Judaism, Christianity and Islam*, positions her at the forefront of the emerging Interspiritual Movement. www.mirabaistarr.com

brother david steindl-rast

Born in Vienna, Austria, David Steindl-Rast studied art, anthropology and psychology, at the Vienna Academy of Fine Arts (M.A.) and the University of Vienna (Ph.D.). In 1953, he joined Mount Saviour Benedictine Monastery, where he is now a senior member. He began studying Zen in the 1960s and became a pioneer in interfaith dialogue. In 1975 he received the Martin Buber Award for his achievements building bridges between religious traditions. His books include *Gratefulness, the Heart of Prayer*, *Deeper than Words* and *99 Blessings*. Currently, Brother David serves as founding advisor of Gratefulness, a Network for Grateful Living.
www.gratefulness.org

michael stillwater

Michael Stillwater is an artist using music for healing. A filmmaker, author and educator, he is co-creator of *Graceful Passages: A Companion for Living and Dying* and founder of Inner Harmony Music and Song Without Borders. His documentary film, *In Search of The Great Song*, explores and celebrates the power of song to reconnect us to our hearts and each other. He lives in Switzerland and tours internationally, offering contemplative retreats and evolutionary song workshops.
www.innerharmony.com

rick strassman

Rick Strassman, MD, is a clinical associate professor of psychiatry at the University of New Mexico School of Medicine. He is the author of *DMT—The Spirit Molecule*, the co-author of *Inner Paths to Outer Space* and the author of the forthcoming *The Soul of Prophecy* (all published by Inner Traditions).
www.rickstrassman.com

gail straub

Gail Straub is the author of the bestselling *Empowerment: The Art of Creating Your Life As You Want It,* the critically acclaimed *The Rhythm of Compassion and* the awarding-winning feminist memoir *Returning to My Mother's House: Taking Back the Wisdom of the Feminine.* A pioneer in the field of empowerment, she co-directs the Empowerment Institute, a school for transformative social change where over the last three decades she has offered her work to tens of thousands of people worldwide. Gail co-founded IMAGINE: A Global Initiative for the Empowerment of Women currently under way in Afghanistan, Jordan, Africa and India.

www.empowermentinstitute.net

www.imagineprogram.net

lama surya das

Lama Surya Das, who the Dalai Lama affectionately calls the "American lama", has spent over forty years studying with the great spiritual masters of Asia. He is an authorized lama in the Tibetan Buddhist order and the founder of the Dzogchen Center. Surya Das is the author of the international bestseller *Awakening the Buddha Within: Tibetan Wisdom for the Western World* and twelve other books, including his latest release, *Buddha Standard Time: Awakening to the Infinite Possibilities of Now.* His blog, "Ask the Lama," can be found at askthelama.com. To see Surya's lecture and retreat schedule, visit www.surya.org.

katherine woodward thomas

Katherine Woodward Thomas is the national bestselling author of *Calling in "The One": 7 Weeks to Attract the Love of Your Life,* a licensed psychotherapist, creator of the *Conscious Uncoupling Program* and co-creator/co-leader of the *Feminine Power* transformative courses for women. Her work has touched the lives of hundreds of thousands of people throughout the world, both through her live and virtual learning communities. As a highly sought-after relationship expert, Katherine is deeply devoted to the evolution of love in our world in all of its many forms.

www.katherinewoodwardthomas.com

donna thomson

Donna Thomson is an intuitive, author and meditation teacher. Since 1987 she has channeled healing light, energy and information for the benefit of others in individual and group awareness sessions. With her husband and partner in healing work, Bob Schrei, she is the co-originator of SourcePoint Therapy®, an energy healing system. Donna is the author of *The Vibrant Life: Simple Meditations to Use Your Energy Effectively* (Sentient Publications, 2006).

www.sourcepointtherapy.com

llewellyn vaughan-lee

Sufi teacher and author Llewellyn Vaughan-Lee, Ph.D., has followed the Naqshbandi Sufi path since he was nineteen. In 1991 he became the successor of Irina Tweedie, author of *Daughter of Fire* and moved to Northern California where he founded the Golden Sufi Center. He has specialized in the area of dreamwork, integrating the ancient Sufi approach to dreams with the insights of Jungian psychology. Since 2000 his writing and teaching have focused on spiritual responsibility in this time of transition, an awakening global consciousness of oneness, the Anima Mundi and spiritual ecology.

www.goldensufi.org

www.workingwithoneness.org

jason apollo voss

Jason authored the 2011 Foreword Reviews Business and Economics Book of the Year finalist, *The Intuitive Investor: A Radical Guide for Manifesting Wealth*, a book about how to make more conscious decisions. Jason retired as co-Portfolio Manager of the Davis Appreciation Fund (DAIF) in 2005 after it bested the NASDAQ by 77.0 percent, the S&P 500 by 49.1 percent and the DJIA by 35.9 percent. Jason has given numerous press interviews but is most proud of being published simultaneously in the *Wall Street Journal* and *New Age Journal* in February 2011. Jason has been meditating since he was seven.

www.jasonapollovoss.com

mark robert waldman

Mark Waldman is a faculty member of the College of Business at Loyola Marymount University in Los Angeles. He coaches individuals in business and personal development and has authored twelve books, including *Words Can Change Your Brain* and *How God Changes Your Brain*, picked by Oprah as one of the nine "must-read" books for 2012. According to *Time, Newsweek* and the *Washington Post,* he and Andy Newberg are the world's leading authorities on spirituality and the brain. His research has been featured in *O* magazine, the *New York Times, Forbes, Entrepreneur* and dozens of other magazines.

www.markrobertwaldman.com

alex warden

Alex Warden is a mystic devoted to answering the call of her heart: to share the experience of the essential oneness of life with others. Her work focuses on the development of relational consciousness, an awareness born from the primordial feminine knowing of unity

and interrelatedness. A mother, spiritual director and the founder of Essential Oneness, Alex speaks and leads workshops and retreats internationally on spirituality, feminine wisdom and dream studies. She has extensive experience in Christian mysticism and has been a student of Sufism since 1996.
www.essentialoneness.org

susun weed

Susun Weed, author and herbalist, is the voice of the Wise Woman tradition, where healing comes from nourishment. She is known internationally as an extraordinary teacher with a joyous spirit, a powerful presence and an encyclopedic knowledge of herbs and health. She restores herbs as common medicine and empowers us all to care for ourselves; she is the author of the Wise Woman Herbal Series, including five books on women's health and wellbeing the Wise Woman Way.
www.susunweed.com

hank wesselman

Dr. Hank Wesselman, Ph.D., is a paleoanthropologist and award-winning author of eight books on shamanism, including *The Spiritwalker Trilogy, Awakening to the Spirit World* (with Sandra Ingerman,) and *The Bowl of Light*, an account of his philosophical discussions with the Hawaiian visionary Hale Makua. He is a shamanic teacher and practitioner now in the thirtieth year of his apprenticeship and resides on Hawai'i Island.
www.sharedwisdom.com

ganga white

Ganga White is the founder of the White Lotus Foundation, and Yoga Ashram, in Santa Barbara, California and is recognized as an outstanding teacher and exponent of Yoga. He has been called one

of the "architects of American yoga" and a "pioneer of yoga" by the *Yoga Journal*. Since 1967 he has made many valuable and enduring contributions to his field. Ganga White is the author of *Yoga Beyond Belief—Insights to Awaken and Deepen Your Practice*.
www.whitelotus.org

marcia wieder

Marcia Wieder, CEO/Founder of Dream University, is leading a Dream Movement. Whether teaching at the Stanford Business School, speaking to executives in China or addressing young women at Girl Scout Camp, her riveting style impacts audiences worldwide. She is the personal Dream Coach to Jack Canfield, stars in *Beyond the Secret* with Bob Proctor and is a member of the Transformational Leadership Council, along with John Gray and Marianne Williamson. She has authored fourteen books and appeared on *Oprah*, *Today* and in her own PBS-TV special.
www.dreamuniversity.com

terry tempest williams

Terry Tempest Williams has been called "a citizen writer"—a writer who speaks out eloquently on behalf of an ethical stance toward life. Her writing has appeared in *The New Yorker*, the *New York Times*, *Orion* magazine and numerous anthologies worldwide as a crucial voice for ecological consciousness and social change. She has also published several books, including *Refuge: An Unnatural History of Family and Place*, *Red: Passion and Patience in the Desert*, *An Unspoken Hunger: Stories From the Field*, *Leap; Finding Beauty in a Broken World* and *When Women Were Birds*. She and her husband, Brooke Williams, divide their time between Castle Valley, Utah, and Jackson Hole, Wyo.
www.coyoteclan.com

Marianne Williamson is an internationally acclaimed spiritual teacher. Six of her 10 published books have been *New York Times* bestsellers. Four of these have been #1 *New York Times* bestsellers. *A Return to Love* is considered a must-read of the New Spirituality. One paragraph from that book, beginning, "Our deepest fear is not that we are inadequate. Our deepest fear is that we are powerful beyond measure..."–which is often misattributed to Nelson Mandela's Inaugural address–is considered an anthem for a contemporary generation of seekers. Marianne's latest *New York Times* bestseller is *A Course in Weight Loss: 21 Spiritual Lessons for Surrendering Your Weight Forever. A Course in Weight Loss* was selected by Oprah as one of her "Favorite Things" in 2010.

www.marianne.com

fred alan wolf

Fred Alan Wolf, Ph.D., works as a physicist, writer and lecturer. His work in quantum physics and consciousness is well known through his popular and scientific writing. He is the author of sixteen books and audio CDs, many technical and popular articles and is also known as Dr. Quantum. He appeared in many movies, including *What the Bleep Do We Know?* and *The Secret*. He won the National Book Award for *Taking the Quantum Leap*; his latest book is entitled *Time-loops and Space-twists: How God Created the Universe*. www.fredalanwolf.com

carmela "millie" yacoboni

Carmela "Millie" Yacoboni is a daughter, sister, aunt, wife, mother, grandmother and friend to many. Millie is an artist who creates brushless paintings and the author of *4U*, a four-ingredient cookbook, and a fundraiser for children with cleft palates. She lives in Florida and is part of the water aerobics group "Waterlogged Divas." Now 92, she says, "Getting old is great! Look at the alternative."

tom zender

Tom Zender is a successful business executive and mentor, a best-selling author and a recognized spiritual leader. Author of *God Goes to Work* and *One-Minute Meditations at Work*, he raises work and business consciousness for organizational integrity and conscious commerce. He held management positions at General Electric and Honeywell and was a senior vice president in NYSE and NASDAQ listed corporations. Tom is president emeritus of Unity, which serves over three million people of all faiths worldwide. His corporate board experience includes NASDAQ- and Toronto Stock Exchange-listed companies, plus nonprofits that include the Evolutionary Leaders, the Forum for Corporate Directors and Ottawa University. www.tomzendermentor.com

zuleikha

Zuleikha is an international performer, social activist, self-care trainer and teacher in the art of movement. Renowned for her global work with women and girls, her "storydance" performances and Rumi Concert collaborations, she is a recipient of the Images and Voices of Hope Media Award for her outstanding work in the world promoting positive personal and social change. www.storydancer.com

about the editor

celeste yacoboni is passionate about helping people discover a deeper experience of the sacred in their daily lives. Ordained as a Minister of Walking Prayer by the Center for Sacred Studies, Celeste leads "How Do You Pray?" workshops in which people share and experience different ways of connecting to a Source greater than themselves. She also maintains a private practice in Santa Fe, New Mexico where she facilitates healing and transformation through her unique approach to spiritual coaching and her mastery of a number of the healing arts. With breath, touch, prayer and song she holds a space of awareness, presence and inspiration that allows her clients to experience a profound integration of body, mind, spirit and emotion. *How Do You Pray?* is her first book.

www.howdoyoupray.com

photo © jennifer esperanza

permissions

Images

Love and Gratitude Water Crystal, Photograph © Office of Masaru Emoto, LLC.

Cynthia Jurs, Photograph © Jennifer Esperanza/JenniferEsperanza.com.

Daniel Craig, Photograph © Jennifer Esperanza/JenniferEsperanza.com.

Praying, Oil Painting © 1984 Alex Grey/www.cosm.org.

Chaos, Order, Secret Writing, Oil Painting © 2006 Allyson Grey/www.cosm.org.

Medicine Buddha, Thangkaas Painting © Lama Gyurme.

Zuleikha, Photograph © Katie Johnson/www.Katiescamera.net.

Mother of Fairest Love, © William H. McNichols/www.fatherbill.org.

Light Being, Photograph © 1992 Susan Slotter/www.SusanSlotter.com.

Quotes

Bede Griffiths quote, excerpted with kind permission from *The Golden String*, Templegate Publishing, copyright 1954.

Ganga White poem, from *Yoga Beyond Belief: Insights to Awaken and Deepen Your Practice* by Ganga White, published by North Atlantic Books, copyright © 2007 by Ganga White. Reprinted by permission of publisher.

Rumi quote, copyright © Coleman Barks, *The Essential Rumi*

Printed in the USA
CPSIA information can be obtained
at www.ICGtesting.com
JSHW012048140824
68134JS00035B/3327